# CHAMPIONSHIP
# BASKETBALL
## by **12** GREAT COACHES

E.A. Diddle       Bill Gardiner       Ed Jucker       John B. McLendon,

Hank Iba       Ken Norton       Brian McCall       John W. Bunn

PRENTICE-HALL INC., Englewood Cliffs, New Jersey

Eddie Hickey          Ray Mears          Ben Carnevale          John R. Wooden

# CHAMPIONSHIP
# BASKETBALL
## by **12** GREAT COACHES

### COMPILED & EDITED BY

### HARDIN McLANE

CHAMPIONSHIP BASKETBALL
BY 12 GREAT COACHES
Hardin McLane

© 1965, by

PRENTICE-HALL, INC.

Englewood Cliffs, New Jersey

Library of Congress
Catalog Card Number: 66-10955

PRINTED IN THE UNITED STATES OF AMERICA
12650—BC

*To my two head coaches and most loyal fans —*

**Marilyn and Michelle**

# ABOUT THIS BOOK . . .

This book is taken from a series of tape-recorded interviews with the twelve contributing coaches. It is different than most basketball books in that it presents coaching strategy from twelve of the great coaches of the game, rather than limiting itself to the ideas of a single man. The coaches represented here have already contributed much to basketball, and their thoughts printed here represent a further contribution.

It has been a pleasure to work and talk with these coaches and I trust that the book will provide assistance for coaches of basketball on every level of play. At one time, a new coach had to learn everything by trial and error, but today, through books like this one, he can benefit by the wisdom and experience of the greatest coaches the game has produced.

# *ACKNOWLEDGEMENTS*

My sincere thanks to all who played a part in the preparation of this book—the 12 contributing coaches who proved their greatness by consenting to share some of the ideas that have made them great; my wife, Marilyn McLane, for so many things too numerous to mention; the typists, Marilyn Wiseman, Rosemary Jenkins, and Diane Elmore; to Dee Huddleston and his staff at Radio Station WIEL for the use of their facilities; to my fellow teachers at Elizabethtown Catholic High School; and to Tom Ecker, who was the first to conceive the idea for this type of book.

# *INTRODUCTION*

By Earl Cox
Assistant Sports Editor
*The Courier-Journal,* Louisville, Kentucky

In Kentucky, where high-school basketball is king, the crown prince is Hardin McLane.

Successful as a coach and real estate agent, McLane now directs his talents to picking the brains of the best coaches in college basketball. *Championship Basketball by Twelve Great Coaches,* edited by McLane, is certain to be the most valuable book ever written on basketball coaching.

Colorful Ed Diddle, who gained fame as coach at Western Kentucky State College, rightfully occupies a prominent spot in this book. The 31-year-old McLane served as manager of Diddle's Hilltopper teams for four years and gained much of his basketball knowledge from "Uncle Ed."

McLane's 189-47 won-lost record during seven years as coach at Elizabethtown Catholic High School is impressive by any standard. And it becomes somewhat phenomenal when one considers the caliber of competition and the enrollment of Catholic High School. McLane's superbly drilled players represent a student body of less than 100 boys. And yet they win consistently against schools with enrollments of over 2,000.

McLane's colleagues have honored him with numerous Coach-of-the-Year awards, and he has twice been the recipient of sportsmanship awards from officials' groups.

Because of a lucrative real estate business which he conducts in his spare time and during summer months, McLane has spurned attractive offers from larger schools.

McLane has put as much zeal into this book as he has into coaching and business. Coaches—and fans who desire a richer appreciation of basketball—have much to gain from this book.

# CONTENTS

Quarter Court Man-to-Man Press • Half-Court Man-
to-Man Press • Zone Presses • Philosophy of the
Press

Offset the Strength of Your Opponent • Two Methods
of Stopping the Fast Break • Playing the Slow Game
• Stopping the Outlet Pass • Other Things to Consider When Pressing • Man-to-Man Press • Defensing the Fast Break When Outnumbered Under the
Opponent's Goal • Mental Attitude

Reasons for the Press • The Press Is Making Us
Coach Better • To Beat the Press • How Oklahoma
State Attacks the Press • Attack #1 • Attack #2—
Against the Man-to-Man Press • Attack #3—Against
the Zone Press

Three Basic Situations • A Common Error—Over-
Coaching • Simple, Yet Fluid • Tip-off Plays • In-
Bounds Plays • Stall Plays

Charting • Who Should Keep Charts? • Game
Charts • Shot Chart • Turnovers • Rebound Chart
• Jump Ball Chart • Official's Chart • Practice
Charts • Foul Shot Charts • Twenty-one • One-on-

# CHAMPIONSHIP
# BASKETBALL
## by 12 GREAT COACHES

E. A. Diddle, the recently retired coach of the Western Kentucky "Hilltoppers," will go down in athletic history as one of the most colorful figures the sports world has ever known. He has become famous for his antics with the red towel that is his constant companion on the bench. Never done as a show, the towel-tossing started as a nervous habit. It soon became a trade mark of Western's great coach and a revered tradition at the college.

Diddle is a firm believer in basketball fundamentals, and he imparts

# E. A. Diddle

this belief to his players. He advocates a fast style of play, accompanied by topnotch conditioning.

Under Diddle's guidance, Western has played against the nation's best collegiate basketball teams. His teams have competed in the Olympic play-offs and in such prestige-laden tournaments as the NCAA, National Invitational, Sugar Bowl, Orange Bowl, Bluegrass, All-College, Kentucky Invitational, and National Campus. In addition, Diddle is the only man ever to compile over 700 victories in more than 1000 games at one college.

The Hilltoppers have practically monopolized championships of all three conferences to which they have belonged. The collection of titles includes 13 in the Kentucky Intercollegiate Athletic Association. In addition, the Hilltoppers have won or shared the Ohio Valley Conference Championship 11 times in the 16 year history of the league.

A major factor in Diddle's success has been his unique talent for recognizing potential in young players. Diddle is zealously proud of his players and holds for each of them an affection equalling that which he has for the game of basketball itself. Well over 100 of his former players are now coaching in both the high school and college ranks.

1

# THE OFFENSIVE
# FUNDAMENTALS
# IN BASKETBALL

E. A. Diddle
Basketball Coach (Ret.)
Western Kentucky State College

Fundamentals *are* basketball. It is only through the mastery of shooting, passing, jumping, pivoting, running, dribbling, body balance, feinting, and faking that one can have a good basketball team. We are not doing our job properly as coaches unless we spend a great deal of time on these major aspects of the game.

If a player is a good fundamentalist and he has the desire and the physical equipment with which to play, he should be a good ball player. Knowledge of fundamentals will lead a player to the poise, relaxation, and confidence that is necessary to get the job done. You must work on *all* fundamentals. If a player can do only one thing well, he is only part of a basketball player.

Fundamental drills should be related to the types of offense and defense used. For instance, if you are using a fast break offense, your fundamental drills should be geared to that type of offense. If you use a pressing defense, your drills should be selected to improve that facet of the game. But no matter what drills you choose, spend a great deal of time on them. The player well versed in fundamentals is usually going to do a much better job than the boy who plays more or less by ear.

Practice sessions should never be draggy; the players should leave the floor wanting more. This is where the wise use of fundamental drills will improve your practice sessions.

The larger part of our fundamental drills are performed on a competitive basis. There is nothing that can take the place of the kind of competition that occurs when two boys get together and try to execute their fundamentals and see which one can do the job better. We use many drills where we have one-on-one, two-on-two, three-on-three, rebounding, shooting, or working on any other phase of the game that we feel needs work.

### SHOOTING

The good shooters are those boys who have started early, have a good eye for the basket, have good hands, and have worked at it so much that it becomes easy for them. I don't think everyone can learn to be a *great* shooter, but I do think that if a boy has a large amount of desire for the game, and if he has all the other attributes of a good basketball player, he can become a *good* shooter by working at it diligently.

I am sure you will find that all the outstanding shooters spent long hours shooting at the basket and are smart enough to analyze their own shortcomings and correct them. I don't think shooters are born; they are made through great desire and hard work. A player must develop confidence. He must believe that his shot will go into the basket. If he should happen to miss, he must feel sure that he will hit his next one.

### LENGTH OF SHOOTING DRILLS

We spend about 30 minutes each day in shooting practice. Each player has his own ball, and he practices shooting from the place on the floor where he shoots the most during a game. We let him do this for 15 or 20 minutes and then begin our formal shooting drills. We use several different drills and rotate them from day to day to keep the practice from becoming dull.

Repetition is one of the most important aspects of learning, and we carry this principle into all our drills. One of the most important things for a new basketball coach to remember is that doing things over and over again plays a major role in any success he might have.

Impress upon your boys that they must give their best each day in practice; for as they practice, so will they play. If they try hard in practice, they will automatically play hard in the game.

### What to Shoot At

Not many players know what they are shooting at. We even run into them in college. They do not know whether they should be shooting at the back of the rim, just over the nearest rim, or at the backboard. We teach our players to shoot the ball rather softly and just get the ball to the basket. We want the boys to shoot just over the nearest rim and never hit the backboard. Most boys worry about their shots falling short, but we would rather have the shot fall short than hit the backboard, because we can easily correct that by having the boy shoot a little higher or a little harder. We also want the boys to have a little backspin on the ball because this means they have good control and that it is just coming off the tips of their fingers.

The one time we want the boys to use the backboard is on the three- or four-foot, side angle, crip shots. At this angle and distance we feel that this greatly improves their chances of hitting the shot. But we never want the boys to use the backboard for the 10 or 15 footer. Usually, when a boy hits a long bank shot he has been lucky, and he knows it. If you watch carefully, you will see him suppress a small smile.

## How to Handle the Unorthodox Shooter

At times, the high school coach will be faced with the problem of the unorthodox shooter. Should he attempt to change the boy's shooting? Or if he is a fairly good shot, should he leave his shooting alone?

After 41 years of coaching basketball, I feel the following policy is best in the majority of cases. The basketball player who still gets the job done and hits a good percentage in spite of unorthodox shooting habits probably should be left alone. If it is some minor thing and you have found by working with the boy that it is beyond his control, you may be doing both the boy and your team an injustice by trying to change his shooting style. If you cut down on his point production and cause yourself to lose several ball games, you will be taking a backward step rather than progressing.

Several years ago, we had a player who was not shooting a two-hand set shot "the right way." His hands were so large that they overlapped on the ball. We suddenly realized that, by requiring him to shoot a two-hand set shot the way everybody else did, we were cutting down on this player's point production and, thereby, endangering our chances of winning. Adjustments were made, and the boy ended up shooting the old midwestern push from the guard position. With his left hand underneath the ball for support, he would shoot a long, one-hand push shot. Needless to say, after this player, Tom Marshall, went on to become an All-American, we certainly were happy we decided against requiring him to shoot the conventional two-hand set shot.

If, on the other hand, you have a player who has an unorthodox shot and is not hitting for a good percentage, then I think you should work with him to change his shooting so he will be more productive.

SHOOTING DRILLS

*Around the World* (Figure 1-1). Divide the team into two groups, with half on each end of the floor. The better shooters should be on one end, and the poorer shooters on the other end to make competition even. The first shooter starts under the basket and keeps shooting until he misses. Then the rest of the shooters follow in turn. If a player misses, he may stay at his present position or "take a chance" and shoot a second shot from that position. If he hits the second shot, he continues to the

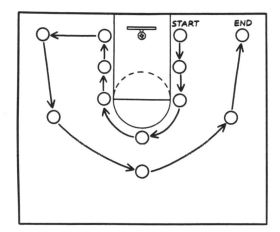

**Figure 1-1 Around the World.**

next position. If he misses his chance, he goes back to the starting point. The first player to go all the way "around the world" and hit the right-corner shot is the winner.

*Team 21* (Figure 1-2). Divide the team into two groups, with each group having a ball. On the command "start" from the coach, the front man in each line starts shooting. A long shot counts two points, and a short shot one point. Boys must shoot short shots from the spot they rebound the long shot. After shooting long and short shots, the shooter passes to the next man in his line and goes to the rear of the line. The coach keeps score aloud, with the first team to score 21 points winning. Play two out of three games in all three positions. (A, B, C.)

*Bump Drill* (Figure 1-3). This drill teaches players to concentrate on the shot, even though they may be fouled or "bumped" in the game while shooting. This drill may be used in practicing crip shots or jump shots. The arrows in the illustration show various approaches to the basket. The coach stands near the spot from which the player will shoot the ball. Shooters dribble by the coach one at a time and go up for their shots. The coach slightly pushes shooters' hips or shoulders as they shoot the ball. Players soon learn to disregard the "bump" and concentrate on making the shot.

*Shooting Over Screen Drill* (Figure 1-4). This drill provides good experience for players in learning to shoot over a teammate's screen. Forwards can screen for guards' shots, or guards can screen for forwards' shots.

## FREE THROWS

Foul shooting is a very serious business, and few people know how much time to spend shooting free throws in practice. We have made a number of surveys with our own teams, but I don't think we have proved anything.

We have had some ball clubs that spent very little time practicing foul shooting and, yet, were great foul shooters in the game. On the other hand, we have had ball clubs with which we

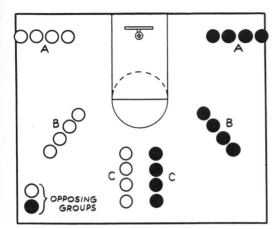

Figure 1-2   Team 21.

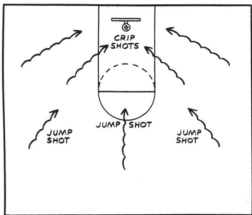

Figure 1-3   Bump Drill.

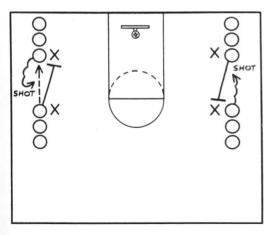

Figure 1-4   Shooting Over
Screen Drill.

*11*

spent much time working on foul shooting, and yet they were poor foul shooters in the game. Probably all coaches have had that experience, but in the majority of cases we feel that the more time you spend practicing foul shooting, the better your team will hit their foul shots in the game. Because we believe that a good foul-shooting team will win the close games, a great deal of time is spent on free throws at Western.

We think a ballplayer has to be a good shot to be a good foul shooter. But it all goes back to the same prerequisites for any type of fundamentals—poise, confidence, and relaxation. Anyone can improve on his foul shooting if he is willing to work hard at it and if he believes he will hit the greater majority of his foul shots. We don't believe that all boys should be made to shoot alike when foul shooting. We let them shoot their own preferred shot and try to improve on that.

### DRILLS FOR FREE THROWS

We have several methods of practicing foul shooting. First, we make our drills for free throws competitive. The players are either competing against each other or competing against themselves. Second, the boys are not allowed practice in shooting fouls when they are "cold." Fouls are shot only after they have warmed up, after scrimmaging, or perhaps at the end of practice. The boys do not shoot fouls "cold" in a game, so we try to simulate game conditions. Third, we put pressure on the boys when they are practicing foul shooting. They have pressure on them in the game, so why not in practice?

We use several different methods to build up pressure. We have one drill in which we put six boys on each end of the floor. Each boy has to hit three fouls in a row before anyone can leave. In other words, using six boys, that would be 18 free throws in a row before anyone on that end of the floor can shower. This puts pressure on a boy and is good because, as I have just stated, every time he steps to the line in a game, pressure is on him. We use another similar drill. We have each boy shoot seven consecutive fouls. If he misses before he hits seven in a row, we start him over again. When he can hit 7 in a row, we raise it to 10; after 10, we'll raise it to 12, then to 15. When he can hit 15 in a row, we feel that he is a pretty good foul shooter. This drill goes back to our use of pressure. When a boy gets 12 or 13 in a row, the pressure is on him; and every time a boy walks up to the foul line in a ball game, he feels the same kind of pressure.

Another drill a coach could use with success involves our belief of not practicing fouls "cold." Take your 12 varsity boys and put 6 on each end of the floor. Two boys will shoot fouls; two will throw the ball back to the shooters; and the other two are running laps around the playing floor. After two laps, the runners become shooters, the shooters become retrievers, and the retrievers become runners. After two hard laps, the boys' pulse and breathing are faster. This is akin to game conditions. Impress upon your boys not to hurry their foul shots in this drill. If they shoot only two or three shots while the runners are running their two laps, it is more important to hit those two or three than to shoot six or seven and hit only half of them.

## PASSING

There are so many types of passes used in the present day game of basketball that the average high school coach just doesn't find the time available to teach his players to become proficient in all of them. I feel it is much better to do an adequate job of teaching the most common passes than to attempt to teach every type of pass and doing a half-way job of it. We believe the most important passes to teach your team are the bounce pass, the two-hand overhead pass, the two-hand chest pass, and the baseball throw used on the fast break.

Of course, there will be occasions when your players will use some other type pass such as the hook pass, flip pass, etc. We feel, however, that the players will be able to use these passes without the coach spending too much time on them.

## PASSING PROBLEMS

We have difficulty with some of our freshmen wanting to lob the ball, but we soon rid them of that. We want them to throw the ball with snap and speed and not use the lazy lob pass.

We don't go in much for fancy passing. We tell our boys not to throw the behind the back pass even if they are good at it, unless it is the only pass they can use. If they can pass the ball some other way, we prefer that they do because the use of the fancy pass looks as if the player is grandstanding or trying to be the whole show, and we don't want boys to do that.

Peripheral vision drills help a team's passing, but we do not advocate a lot of blind passing. We do want our boys to fake one way and throw another. Boys telegraphing their passes can be the difference between winning and losing a ball game. We do not use the head fake alone when attempting to pass the ball. We want our players to use their head, eyes, hands, feet, or the dipping of their shoulders, and not just the moving of their head.

One fake we have always thought useless is the boy driving to the baseline or the sideline and faking outside where there is nothing but the boundary line and rows of spectators. We tell our boys that no one can come out of the crowd and guard them, so this is a useless fake.

### RECEIVING THE PASS

We want our players to move and meet the ball. All a very

good ball player needs is the sight of the ball in flight, and he will catch it. But we like the boys to have a good hand spread and to reach forward. When the ball touches the hand, we also like them to give a little as in catching a baseball. Tell your players they must catch the pass before they can do anything with the ball. Some boys make the mistake of trying to throw the ball before they catch it and, as a result, fumble a great deal. Other boys hold their hands and wrists too stiff, and naturally they do a lot of fumbling. Some have difficulty gripping the ball. I think a player should receive the ball with the tips of his fingers and try to keep the palm of his hand off the ball.

### RELATE DRILLS TO OFFENSE

As part of our plan to relate our fundamental drills to the offense and defenses used, our offense is worked into our passing drills. By doing this, our players are not only working on their fundamentals, but they also are getting the feel of our offense. Not all of our passing drills are directly related to our offense, but we do try to use a number of them when it is possible.

### PASSING DRILLS

*Pivoting and Passing Drill* (Figure 1-5). Number one in all three lines dribbles out to the foul line and does a jump stop;

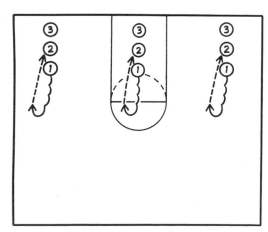

**Figure 1-5  Pivoting and Passing Drill.**

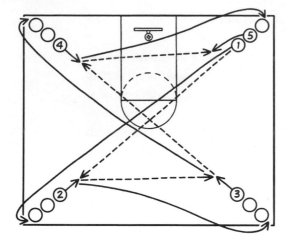

Figure 1-6  Figure-8 Passing Drill.

then, he does either a right or left rear pivot and passes to number two. The number one man then goes to the rear of the line, and number three moves up to receive the pass from number two and continues the drill.

*Figure-8 Passing Drill* (Figure 1-6). Number one passes to two and follows the pass, going to his right; two passes to three and goes to his right; three passes to four and goes to his left; four passes to five and goes to his left. All above movements are repeated. Each receiver meets the pass.

*Bull in the Ring* (Figure 1-7). Five players form a circle with a defensive player in the middle. Any pass may be used in this drill. If a defensive player intercepts or deflects a pass, he ex-

Figure 1-7  Bull in the Ring.

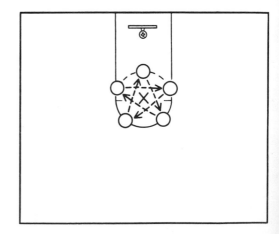

changes places with the passer. Passers cannot pass ball to the man next to them on circle, but must pass to teammate across the circle.

## DRIBBLING

A good dribbler should be able to dribble with his fingers and not with the palm of his hand. There are a number of little gimmicks out now that you can utilize to prevent your players from using their palms, such as gloves with padded palms.

### TECHNIQUE

In dribbling with your right hand, the ball should be slightly to the right of your right foot and about five or six inches to the front. A good dribbler will not bounce the ball directly in front of him. He will push, or "finger," the ball rather than bat the ball with his hand. He will be able to stop on a dime and change his pace in any direction. The only way a player learns to accomplish all this is by practice, practice, and more practice.

A good dribbler will protect the ball by keeping his body between the ball and his opponent. He will reverse his dribble, fake right, and drive left. It takes an intelligent and capable boy to do this kind of dribbling, but it can be done.

We like a boy to dribble fairly low for deception when confronted by the defensive man. When in the open, during the fast break for instance, he should dribble higher for speed. We don't like a boy to pitter-patter the ball or turn his back to the defense on the dribble. The dribbler who turns his back to the defensive man is going to have the ball stolen from him many times.

Don't let your boys dribble with their head and eyes down. This habit prevents their seeing teammates who are in the open

for a shot. We use many drills at Western to improve our dribbling. We dribble around chairs, play dribble tag, speed dribble,
and use several dribble-shooting or dribble-passing combination
drills.

## DRILLS FOR DRIBBLING

*Dribble, Reverse, Drive, and Shoot Drill* (Figure 1-8). No. 1
dribbles forward, then left, does a reverse dribble, and drives
for lay-up shot. He then goes to rear of line 2. Man number 2

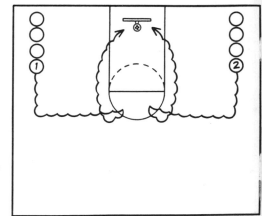

**Figure 1-8   Dribble, Reverse,
Drive, and Shoot Drill.**

dribbles forward, then right, does a reverse dribble, and drives
for lay-up shot. He then goes to rear of line 1.

*Speed Dribble Drill* (Figure 1-9). This is a full-court, competitive drill in which the coach divides team into two groups.
Half of Group A players go to the far end of the floor, and the
other half remains on the close end. Group B does the same.
Player number 1 in each group has a ball. On the command
"Start" from the coach, these first men "speed dribble" to their
teammates on the other end of the floor, pass the ball to the

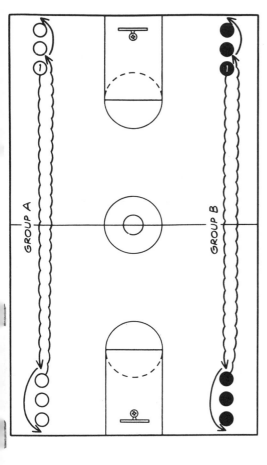

Figure 1-9  Speed Dribble Drill.

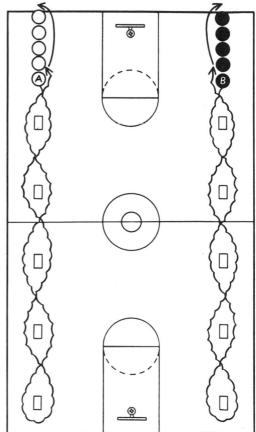

Figure 1-10  Chair Drill.

first man in the line and go to the end of that line. The drill is completed when number 1 players return to their original positions.

*Chair Drill* (Figure 1-10). This is a full-court, competitive drill in which the squad is divided into two groups. An equal

number of chairs is set up on each side of the floor. The first
man in each line has a ball. On the command "Start" from the
coach, they dribble in and out of all the chairs, return, and then
pass the ball to the next man in line. The first team to return
all players to original positions is the winner.

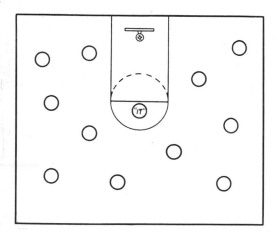

Figure 1-11   Dribble Tag.

*Dribble Tag* (Figure 1-11). This drill may be either full or
half court. All of the players have a ball and must stay within
the confines of the playing floor. One player is "it" and must
tag any of the other players. The drill is performed in the same
manner as any tag game, with the exception that all players
must be dribbling a ball at all times.

### REBOUNDING

Here at Western, good rebounding is of the utmost importance.
With our fast-break and high-scoring games there are naturally
more shots taken and, therefore, more rebounds than in a slower
type game. We teach our boys that the team that controls the
boards will win the majority of the time.

Rebounding, like defense, is a facet of the game in which the unproductive scorer can become a valuable asset to the team. Although the ability to rebound effectively comes more naturally to some players than to others, it is a basketball skill that all boys can learn.

## YOU'VE GOT TO HAVE GUTS

Intestinal fortitude plays a major role in rebounding. Action gets rugged at times under the boards, and the boy unwilling to get in there and "scrap" will not be an effective rebounder. You must instill in your boys the fact that it often takes the second, third, or even fourth effort to obtain the ball. They must take pride in their rebounding ability just as the high scorer takes pride in his scoring ability. Too many times we ignore the good rebounder in favor of the "star" who scores many points in a game. If you give trophies at the end of the season, include a trophy for the top rebounder. When talking to the press or fans, give as much praise to your rebounders as to your scorers. Before long, the players who can't become high scorers will begin to realize that they, too, are appreciated. If you praise these boys, the press and fans will follow suit.

## TECHNIQUE

In defensive rebounding, players must hesitate momentarily to see in which direction their opponents are moving to reach the goal. The defensive men must then pivot in that direction to block out your players when they are on offense. You must have your boys fake one way and go the other. Have them fake left and go right, fake right and go left, or fake right and left, then go right. This must be done quickly, since there are only a few seconds available to accomplish this.

We like a boy to be in a comfortable jumping position, to keep his head up, elbows out, hands cupped ready for the ball, and knees bent. He should be in a crouched position, but not too low, and should take up as much room under the boards as comfort permits. The good rebounder will use his buttocks to good advantage when his blocked-out opponent tries to get in front of him under the basket.

Have your boys jump forward rather than straight up when rebounding. This will prevent their being tied up or having the ball slapped out of their hands.

The rebounder should land with his knees spread and elbows extended to protect the ball. Also, with all the bumping that goes on under the boards in this modern game of basketball, the rebounder landing with his feet comfortably spread will not be forced to travel with the ball when contact occurs. When the rebounder lands with his feet too close together, he is apt to lose his footing and travel with the ball upon contact with an opponent.

Timing is very important. Too many boys jump too soon or too late. As in every part of the game, timing takes practice.

### METHODS OF IMPROVEMENT

We do a number of things both offensively and defensively to improve our rebounding. Sometimes we drill without a ball and at other times with a ball. In one of our drills without a ball, we place six men under the basket, three in defensive position, and the other three in their normal offensive positions. The defensive players are instructed to block out and hold their opponents when the coach blows his whistle. On the second whistle, the defensive men turn and get ready to jump as if a shot had just been taken. All this time, the offensive players in the drill have been trying to get in front of the men attempting to block them out. Later, we add a ball to the drill and discontinue the use of the whistle. We use the same three-on-three formation, but we place a manager or substitute player out front with no defense on him. The three offensive players and the manager move the ball around, with any one of the four shooting the ball at any time. With the shot, the three defensive players attempt to block their opponents from the basket. In both drills we rotate the players, with the offensive and defensive players changing positions. A lot of our offensive and defensive rebounding practice is done in this three-on-three manner. Of course, in both of the above drills you can use ten men—five on offense and five on defense— and obtain the same results. Players also get practical rebounding practice when they are scrimmaging or working at shooting drills.

Our rebounding drills are pretty rough work, but the boys soon learn to like them. The timid boy soon learns that rebounding is a matter of contact, and he just has to go after the ball with everything he has. That is about the only way it can be done. There is no easy way.

*Rebounding Drill* (Figure 1-12). The three offensive players and the manager pass the ball around with anyone shooting at

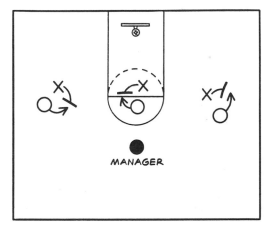

**Figure 1-12   Rebounding Drill.**

any time. The defensive players attempt to block out the offensive players. Upon direction of the coach, the offensive and defensive players can change places.

## SUMMARY

In summary, it is the opinion of both Ted Hornback, my assistant coach for more than 25 years, and myself, that no matter whether you are coaching a grade school team or a professional team, you must spend a great deal of time on fundamentals if you are to enjoy a successful coaching career.

In addition to spending much time on fundamentals, you must do two other things to become an outstanding coach. One is to be a keen student of the game; always try to improve yourself. Attend coaching clinics, talk basketball with other coaches, and read and study any written material on basketball you can find. The other is to instill in your players that priceless attribute— desire. I don't think that one can be a great ball player unless he has desire.

A young man has to want to play; he has to have a great deal of pride and want to do his best. Of course, it means that he must give up some things and make some sacrifices during the basketball season. He has to get more rest than the average student. He has to miss some of the social activities because of training rules. But the boy with desire who wants to be a member of a great basketball team is willing to make these sacrifices. He knows the teams that win the championships are the type of ball clubs that are made up of boys with desire. Members of these teams want to win badly enough to give up those things that are unimportant to the boy during the season.

During the 1961-62 basketball season, we had a player with this type of desire. Bobby Rascoe, an All-American player here at Western, did not have the physical equipment that a great ball player must have. He had very bad feet; he was not a very large boy; he did not have great speed. But he came to play, and he was a coach's dream. You never had to keep after him in practice, because he wanted to be great. I think Bobby's great desire got him where he is today in basketball and made him an All-American.

When Rascoe stepped on the basketball court, he exemplified the perfect basketball player. He was confident, relaxed, and had a great deal of poise because he knew he was a master of his fundamentals. He knew the job to be done and had the desire to do it.

This is the type of ball player all of us, as coaches, want to send out to represent our schools. The way to develop this type player is to remember that fundamentals are definitely a must. I think the best way to answer the question "what role do fundamentals play in basketball?" is to refer to the first sentence in this chapter—*fundamentals are basketball.*

Bill Gardiner came to Loyola University of
the South in 1959. He served for 13 years
as head coach of Spring Hill College in
Mobile, Alabama, building the school into one of the nation's leading
small college cage powers.

In 1954 his Spring Hill club defeated Florida and Georgia to win the
Gator Bowl title, and in 1956 his Badgers defeated Clemson and Mem-
phis State to capture Senior Bowl honors. Spring Hill repeated as
Senior Bowl champs in 1957.

# Bill Gardiner

Gardiner, who received his Master of Arts degree from Maryland in 1952, is a member of the board of directors of the National Association of Collegiate Basketball Coaches and is chairman for District 3 of the Basketball Hall of Fame Committee.

## 2

# LOYOLA'S ISOMETRIC BASKETBALL PROGRAM

Bill Gardiner
Basketball Coach
Loyola University, New Orleans

With coaches trying everything to better their basketball program nowadays, many are turning to isometrics. *Iso* means "the same," and *metric* means "length." Therefore, in this form of exercise nothing moves, but a large amount of energy is expended. Since one of the most important attributes of a basketball player is the possession of explosive power, and isometrics is the best method of developing explosive power, we felt that the use of isometrics would be of tremendous help in our basketball program here at Loyola. We installed the isometrics program several years ago, and we feel that it has been of great help.

Our boys are requested to do the following exercises five days per week until October 15. They should do the exercises before going out on the basketball floor during the off-season work. Starting October 15, we use the reduced exercise program three days per week; this is done after practice rather than before. We would like to have the boys do these exercises 12 months out of the year. We measure every boy at two-week intervals and keep a record of his progress. In addition, every two weeks we check their squat-jump and record this also.

The purpose of these exercises is to increase the strength and jumping ability of the players in the shortest workout period possible. Isometric exercises require less time than does weight lifting. In addition, these exercises can be done alone, whereas weight lifting should be done in pairs. (When using heavy weights, many exercises require that the weights be handed to the person performing the exercise after he has taken the proper position.)

In addition, some other points of our isometric program are listed below.

1.  All exercises are to be done five days per week before and after the actual basketball season. Do all exercises only one time each day.
2.  Calisthenics may be used as a warm-up before going into the exercises. Examples would be: running in place, push-ups, touching toes, knee bends, etc.
3.  In performing the exercises, take 2 seconds to ease into the exercise and then push or pull as hard as possible for 8 seconds.
4.  Take a deep breath and hold it while doing all the exercises. If at any time while in the exercise dizziness occurs, start breathing at once.
5.  During the basketball season, do exercises 1, 4, 6, 7 only. These exercises are to be done two days per week only.
6.  Remember that you only receive benefits from these exercises in proportion to your effort and regularity. At the end of the basketball season, it will be too late to wish that you had done them.

### EXPLANATION OF ILLUSTRATIONS

PRESS. (Figure 2-1). Set bar about hair level (judge this by keeping upper arm parallel to ground), look straight ahead, feet shoulder width apart, palms, facing away from body,

Figure 2-1   Press.

hands shoulder width apart; lock leg, hip, and back muscles.
Look straight ahead and push up.

ARM PULL. (Figure 2-2). Shoulders back, set bar so that it
can be grasped with arms slightly bent, palms facing towards
the body, hands shoulder width apart, feet shoulder width
apart, look up slightly, *pull by rising on toes.* Hold the arms
in the slightly bent position throughout the exercise.

Figure 2-2   Arm Pull.

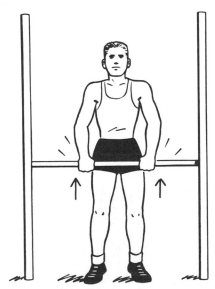

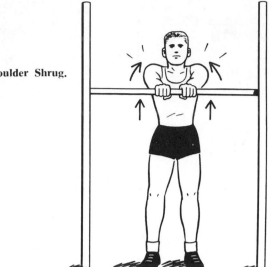

Figure 2-3 Shoulder Shrug.

SHOULDER SHRUG. (Figure 2-3). Grasp bar with arms fully
extended, palms facing body, hands 4 inches apart, feet shoulder width apart, look up, *force shoulders forward and up,
trying to put shoulders in your ears.*

DEAD LIFT. (Figure 2-4). Set bar about knee level when you
are holding hands shoulder width apart, palms facing the
body. Keep head up, hips down, back flat, knees bent, feet
under bar. Pull up through the long axis of the back.

Figure 2-4 Dead Lift.

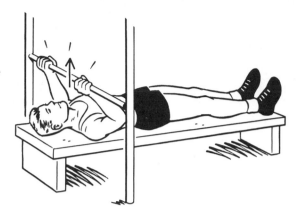

Figure 2-5　Bench Press.

BENCH PRESS. (Figure 2-5). Lie on bench with bar directly over eyes and about 10 inches or 12 inches above the head. Grasp bar with hands about shoulder width apart, palms facing away from body. *Keep back and legs on bench* and push up with arms only. This will give additional arm and shoulder strength.

HEEL RAISE. (Figure 2-6). Bar is set on pads just behind knees with heels ¼ inch to ½ inch off floor. Sit on bench so that knees are directly under bar and feet are directly under knees. Grasp bench with hands, feet shoulder width apart, *raise heels and push up*.

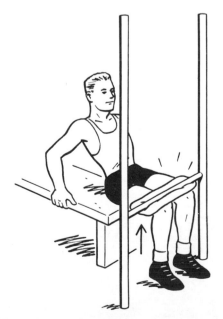

Figure 2-6　Heel Raise.

Figure 2-7   Leg Press.

LEG PRESS. (Figure 2-7). Lie on bench, grasp bench with hands, put feet on bar with legs on a slight angle (not directly under bar). Keep pelvis and back on bench and *raise head up off bench, pushing chin down to chest and pushing with legs.*

SHINS. (Figure 2-8). Sit on edge of bench with legs extended under bar, toes pointed. Bar is about bench level or slightly above. Hook feet under bar, lean body back, grasp bench with hands, head up, feet almost together, and raise bar with legs.

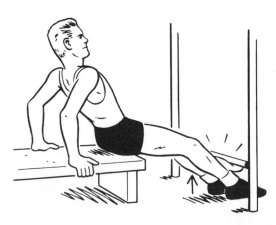

Figure 2-8   Shins.

HAMSTRINGS. (Figure 2-9). Lie face down on bench. Knees are extended over edge of bench, and bar is about 8 inches above height of bench. Hook heels under bar, hold head up, feet are almost together, lift bar with legs.

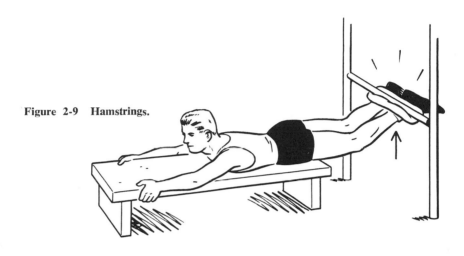

**Figure 2-9   Hamstrings.**

GROAN. (Figure 2-10). Sit on bench and place your arm between your legs with your palm pushing against the inside of one leg and the back of upper arm pushing against the inside of other leg. Push against the arm with your legs.

**Figure 2-10   Groan.**

CURL. (Figure 2-11). Bar is placed waist high. Hand is made
into a fist with palms facing each other and shoulder width

Figure 2-11   Curl.

apart. Place fist under bar, look straight ahead, and lift bar
with clenched fist.

HAND AND WRIST. (Figure 2-12). Squeeze balled-up towel one
hand at a time for required time and hold the pressure. (Do
not release and squeeze as is done with a ball.)

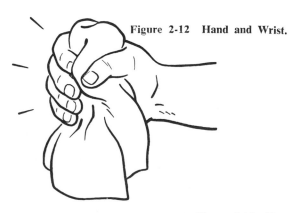

Figure 2-12   Hand and Wrist.

Figure 2-13   Hang.

HANG. (Figure 2-13). Grasp bar with palms facing away from body. Swing freely and gently from side to side and twisting for about 10 seconds and then bring knees up to chest in a frog style kick 5 times. This is not an isometric exercise but is a great overall body builder. But most of all, it pulls out or stretches all the muscles that have been contracted in exercises 1 through 12 and loosens up the body for any basketball that will subsequently be played.

Ed Jucker, the recently retired head coach at the University of Cincinnati, accomplished more in his 5 years as head coach at that school than many achieve in a lifetime.

He directed University of Cincinnati quintets to two consecutive NCAA championships and a second place, three NCAA Midwest regional titles, three Missouri Conference crowns and a Holiday Festival Tournament championship.

Jucker was named "College Basketball Coach of the Year" for both 1961 and 1962 by the Touchdown Club of Columbus, Ohio. His fellow

# Ed Jucker

state coaches voted him the 1963 "Ohio College Coach of the Year" and the personable Bearcat mentor was acclaimed Missouri Valley Conference "Coach of the Year" by his MVC colleagues and by UPI in 1963.

A year earlier Jucker tied for third place in UPI "Coach of the Year" voting and he was fourth in the UPI poll in 1961, his first season as head coach at Cincinnati. That same year he was voted "Missouri Valley Conference Coach of the Year" by the league mentors.

3

# CINCINNATI'S SWING-
# AND-GO OFFENSE*

Ed Jucker
Basketball Coach (Ret.)
University of Cincinnati

———

\* Ed Jucker, *Cincinnati Power Basketball*, 1962, by permission of Prentice-Hall Inc., Englewood Cliffs, N. J.

The backbone of our offensive attack at the University of Cincinnati is our Swing-and-Go series. This pattern and its options evolved from our feeling that the one-on-one situation is highly overrated. Most boys are limited in their natural ability to fake and shoot, which means that the old-fashioned system of sticking the forwards far outside and expecting them to score on the one-on-one is a poor gamble. We prefer to set our players up so they can shoot from well-screened or wide-open positions. Our primary purpose in the Swing-and-Go is to force a switch, freeing our pivot man for a lay-up or close shot. You will notice, however, as this series evolves in the diagrams, that no matter which way the defense commits itself, we have an option that gives us a good screen or an open shot.

I got the germ of this offensive idea watching the professionals roll off a double screen. As far as I know, no other team has an offensive pattern similar to this one. It has proved tremendously successful in our games, and its sheer simplicity makes it almost impossible to stop if opposed by a man-to-man defense.

*41*

### Theory

In the Swing-and-Go the strong-side forward and the pivot man operate as a team only a few steps apart. Since the success of the basic pattern depends upon their reacting together to defensive commitments, it is important that these two men know each other's personal moves as thoroughly as possible. This calls for a great deal of practice together to perfect the timing and screening needed to make this attack work. All shots out of the basic pattern fulfill our demand for close-in shooting.

### An Explanation of the Illustrations in This Chapter

The illustrations that follow have been drawn with clarity in mind. In most cases the offensive team has been identified by letters, and the defensive team by numbers, in an attempt to show the normal positions of the offensive players. (F for forward, P for Pivot, etc.)

The usual method of identifying the strong side and weak side of the court by position of the ball has not been followed for the following reason:

Modern offenses depend to a great extent on an overload of one side of the court since the three-second rule in the foul lane forces the strength of an offense to one side or the other. In the illustrations in which letters are used, therefore, the designation "Strong Side" refers to the overloaded side in the original development of play.

Whenever it has seemed necessary to use the customary (O) and (X) symbols to represent players, I have identified them as offensive or defensive in the text.

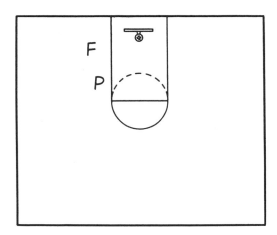

Figure 3-1 The Swing-and-Go Basic Pattern. Positions of forward and pivot.

## BASIC PATTERN

The Swing-and-Go may be set up on either side of the foul lane, although we prefer the left side for a right-handed pivot man. Going into the pattern, the pivot man takes a low post position, and the strong-side forward takes a position several steps behind him (as shown in Figure 3-1). We allow the forward to adjust his position according to the situation; that is, he may move a step or two to the side. He must remain behind the pivot man, however, to set up the play.

In order to receive the ball from the strong-side guard, F must free himself from his defensive man by faking. In Figure

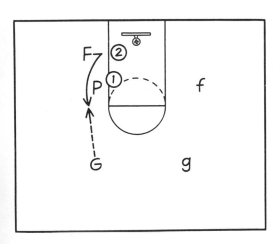

Figure 3-2 The Swing-and-Go Basic Pattern. F drives his man in, then swings off P for the pass from G.

3-2 we show F's fake to take his man as deep as possible, and then his swing back over P. If F's defensive man is playing loose, F can swing back without effort. If his man is playing tight, F must be able to maneuver him in.

F's position when he receives the pass from G should be in front of the pivot man, although a position to the side of P will suffice. The pass is of primary importance. F must receive the

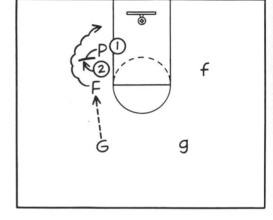

Figure 3-3    The Swing-and-Go Basic Pattern. The defensive man on F (Number 2) has fought through or over the top. F drives to his left, and P picks Number 2.

ball at the end of his swing, then turn and immediately face the basket without using his dribble. His next move is determined by the defense. If his man does not follow him out, he is open for a good shot from where he is. It is surprising how often this simple shot can be taken, especially when F's defensive man is playing loose and finds himself screened out of the play by P and P's defensive man.

In most cases, however, F's defensive man will fight through or work for position by going over the top of P. In these cases F reacts by driving to his left, aided by a pick set up by P (as shown in Figure 3-3). This is the move that is designed to force a switch by the two defensive men involved. If the switch is not made, F continues his drive for an easy shot.

It is important to note here that P must be prepared to set up his pick-screen in two ways. If 2 is beside him, P uses a reverse or back pivot. If defensive man 2 is in front of him, P uses a front pivot. In both cases the right foot is the pivoting foot. (The pivots are shown in Figures 3-15 through 3-18.) Again, I want to emphasize that these moves are reactions to the defense and must be practiced until they become habits. The man who has to stop and think which way he should pivot will not need to pivot at all, unless he wants to look like a dancer without a partner.

Let us assume that the pick is made cleanly, and that as F is driving to his left (Figure 3-3), defensive men 1 and 2 switch. This is the defensive move that we are trying to force. At the instant of switching, the defense is helpless. At that instant, P rolls to the basket, takes a pass from F, and takes a lay-up. This play is our first choice off the Swing-and-Go pattern because, if the defensive men do their jobs perfectly, we score. Figure 3-4 illustrates this option, which we consider the most powerful weapon in our offensive arsenal.

At every step of this series, the defense will dictate our offensive option. For example, the man on P (No. 1 in Figure 3-4)

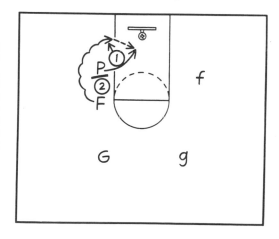

**Figure 3-4** **The Swing-and-Go Basic Pattern.** As F drives to his left, Numbers 1 and 2 switch. On the switch, P immediately rolls to the basket, takes a pass from F, and scores.

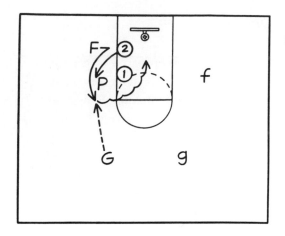

Figure 3-5  The Swing-and-Go Basic Pattern. Number 2 reacts late or is partially picked. F elects to drive around and down the center. If Number 1 switches off to F to prevent this drive, P will roll to the basket and be free for a pass and shot.

may fake the switch and still guard P. That is, No. 1 comes out a step toward F, extending a hand, but he does not pick up F as we wish him to. In this case F does not continue his drive, but takes a close-in shot from the side.

The swing-man, F, must be prepared for one other possibility; namely, a poor defensive reaction to his swing off the pivot man at the beginning of the play. If the defensive man on F is late or partially picked as F comes around for the ball, F may elect to drive on around to the foul line and either shoot from there or continue dribbling down the center to the basket. Figure 3-5 illustrates this option.

If F's drive down the center forces a switch by the defensive

Figure 3-6  The Swing-and-Go Basic Pattern. Number 1 switches after F starts his drive. P rolls to the basket, setting up a quick two-on-one situation.

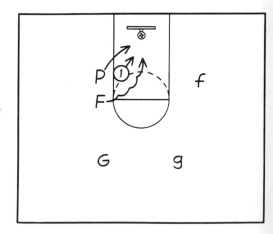

men, P rolls automatically, and the two-on-one situation pictured in Figure 3-6 results.

The success of our Swing-and-Go depends on the weak-side forward's keeping his man busy. If this defensive man is allowed to sag off, he will interfere with the play. To combat this, we tell our weak-side forward to interchange with the weak-side guard or move to the foul line when F starts his drive outside. In running a pattern offense, it is always necessary for the offensive men not directly involved with the ball to have definite assignments that will keep them and their defensive men clear of the play.

Although it is possible for both the strong-side guard and the weak-side guard to make the original pass to the swing-man, F, as he breaks out over the pivot man, we have found a pass from the strong-side guard more desirable. In most modern defenses the man on G will drop off whenever the ball is on the weak side, making a pass from the weak-side Guard to F difficult, if not dangerous. Of course, if G's defensive man still sags excessively even when G has the ball, G must clear out after making the pass to F.

As might be expected, various defenses have been thrown at our Swing-and-Go since we started using it, but the only perfect defense I have seen thus far is the one we ran into during our tour of the Philippines in the summer of 1961.

It is interesting to note here that our games in the Philippines were played according to Olympic rules on courts with a much wider, oblique three-second lane. The boundaries of this lane kept our pivot man and strong-side forward so far outside that the Swing-and-Go lost its effectiveness. It's tough to beat a guy who uses a bucket of paint and a brush. We had to win without much help from the Swing-and-Go, and the experience convinced me that I am not going to advocate any rule change that tampers with the present width of the American three-second lane—not while I have a good pivot man, anyway.

### Continuity off the Swing-and-Go

No pattern offense can be successful if it is made up of set plays that have to be re-set each time they fail to score. Instead, each play has to be part of a general flowing pattern made up of many plays, each of which evolves from any other.

As I have pointed out, Cincinnati's basic Swing-and-Go is a series of preplanned reactions to man-to-man defensive commitments. Many opportunities for good, close-in shots open up as we run this one basic pattern, but we cannot restrict ourselves to these opportunities alone. In other words, we cannot isolate any particular series in our offense either from other patterns or from options off the same basic pattern. To do so would result in a kind of stop-and-go basketball that would be slow to play and dreary to watch. Our Backdoor Trap pattern evolves smoothly from the Swing-and-Go, and vice versa, without any break in the offensive action.

Many factors, such as the defensive positions of our opponents or the offensive instincts of our own players, determine when our patterns should be changed. Effective continuity in the Cincinnati attack is, in the main, the responsibility of our two guards. As they bring the ball up the floor, they are in the best positions to survey the defense and take advantage of any weaknesses they detect. Since our plays are usually keyed by a pass or a cut, we expect our forwards and pivot man to know where the ball is and to be aware of the relative positions of the other men on the floor.

It is my intention to group together all plays run from the basic Swing-and-Go pattern, but I should like you to keep in mind that at any point in our attack before we key one of these plays it is possible for us to break into a new series. With that caution, let us look at some of the continuity we develop directly off the high-low positions of the pivot man and strong-side forward, since these high-low positions are the foundation of this part of our offense.

## GUARD DOUBLE SCREEN

We designed this play for two reasons. First, we felt that we needed a good, close scoring opportunity that could be set up in the closing seconds of the first half or at the end of a tight ball game. Second, our philosophy of team scoring dictates that our guards be given a chance to make baskets from within the tight semicircle in which we do most of our scoring. Never underestimate the importance of providing scoring opportunities for your guards, if you are interested in high team morale.

In setting up this particular play, we make use of the fact that the strong-side forward and the pivot man are only a few steps apart, one behind the other. From these positions it is relatively easy for these men to come together and form a shoulder-to-shoulder screen near the foul lane.

Let us assume that we are nearing the close of the first half, have possession of the ball, and call a time-out. During this time-out, we instruct our team to run the Guard Double Screen for a final shot. With time once again in, our guards bring up the ball while the forwards and pivot man go into their Swing-and-Go positions. The guards come across the center line, and the ball is worked to the strong side.

The weak-side forward keys the play by driving to the foul line for a pass from the strong-side guard. The defensive man on the weak-side guard must glance at the action to his right because it is his responsibility to know where the ball is going, but that glance or look or peek is also an instant of diversion. In that instant the weak-side guard is gone, cutting outside the weak-side forward (as shown in Figure 3-7) and continuing on

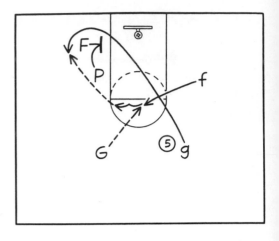

**Figure 3-7 Guard Double Screen.** Here f keys play by going to foul line for a pass from G. When Number 5 looks, g cuts outside f and circles behind the FP double screen. f dribbles to right, then passes in to g.

and around behind the shoulder-to-shoulder double screen set up by F and P. The weak-side forward takes one or two dribbles to his right to get the angle for his pass and then passes in to the weak-side guard. Up and—we hope—in!

This Guard Double Screen is what we call a "bang-bang" play. It breaks fast, and its success depends upon the timing of the cuts and passes. Like all set plays, however, it must be flexible enough to meet various defensive moves. Although our primary aim is to shoot from behind the double screen, I will illustrate various options that we use off this single situation.

Since the key to the Guard Double Screen and its options is not the pass but f's drive to the foul line, the weak-side guard breaks outside F even if the ball is not passed from G to f. If G is forced to hold the ball because he cannot get a pass through, then it is his responsibility to feed the ball to g behind the double screen. G must also be alert to a breakthrough by the defense against the screen. Since such a breakthrough by the man on P or the man on F actually constitutes a switch, P or F will roll on the switch and possibly be open for a pass down the middle from G. (Figures 3-8 through 3-10 show the Guard Double Screen options.)

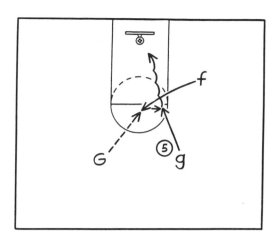

**Figure 3-8  Option—Weak-Side Guard Play.** Hand-off from f to g, who drives in for lay-up.

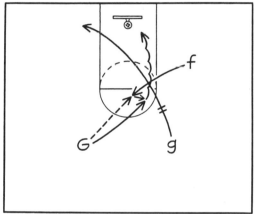

**Figure 3-9  Option — Second Guard Around.** Hand-off from f to g is faked, and f gives to G who follows g around and drives in for lay-up.

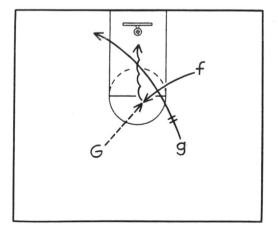

**Figure 3-10  Option — Keeper Play.** f fakes hand-off to g, then rolls and drives in for lay-up.

### FORWARD DOUBLE SCREEN

To take further advantage of the high-low positions of F and P, we have a second set play designed to score in the closing seconds of a half. Again, the strong-side forward and the pivot man go into a shoulder-to-shoulder double screen as the play is keyed, and again, as the play develops, these two men are prepared to roll to the basket if their defensive men prove strong enough to break through or over the top of the screen. This much of the pattern is identical to the Guard Double Screen just described, but here the similarity ends.

For our Forward Double Screen, the guards work the ball to the weak side, and the play unfolds as follows: The weak-side guard, g, passes to the weak-side forward, f, and then follows the ball by moving outside f. Here g stops and takes a return pass from f. This return pass is the key.

The instant f passes back to g, f breaks for the basket and continues on around behind the FP screen. Possibly dribbling once to free himself, g passes across and deep to G who passes in to f behind the screen (as shown in Figure 3-11).

Figure 3-11 **Forward Double Screen.** P a s s is made from g to f. g follows ball, going o u t s i d e . f makes return pass to g and circles behind FP screen. g dribbles f r e e and passes to G, who feeds f behind the screen for a shot.

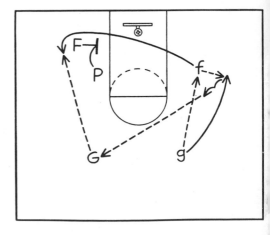

We feel that it is important to have plays of this nature in our repertoire. With seconds to go in a tight ball game, every man on the team needs to know exactly what is expected of him. This is no time to be making up plays in the huddle, or experimenting out on the floor. In such moments of crisis—and there are many of them during a basketball season—there is no substitute for a well-drilled, well-timed set play. Watching such a play work is one of the real rewards of coaching; making it work is one of the real rewards of playing.

Except for the possibility that a strong defensive man may break through or over the screen, there are no other shot options on this particular play. We do instruct our guards, however, to be careful of the long pass from g to G. Should G's defensive man be overplaying, making the pass difficult, G is instructed to drive across the foul line and toward the weak side corner to clear his man. In this case g must continue his dribble out to the front court and make the feed pass to f behind the screen.

I should like to point out here—especially for the benefit of high school players and their coaches—that the dribble is offensive ammunition; it should be used for a definite purpose within the offensive pattern. The pass is the most effective and quickest way to move the ball, and the fewer passes necessary to set up a shot, the better. We strive for a minimum number of passes in setting up a shot, and we try to train our players to respect the dribble, save it for an emergency, and eliminate it whenever possible.

## THE FIVE PLAY

Because the Cincinnati offense gives our guards little opportunity to score from outside, percentages being against long shots off a one-on-one situation, we use plays that bring a guard in for a close shot during our regular attack. (I use the word "regu-

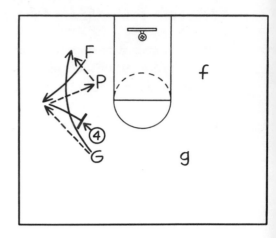

**Figure 3-12  The Five Play.** F breaks to extended foul line and takes pass from G. F passes to P and then cuts to center to pick Number 4, as G cuts outside. P passes to G, who shoots from the cleared area.

lar" here to differentiate between normal floor action and the special spot plays like the Guard Double Screen and the Forward Double Screen.) Too often, normal floor action relegates the guard to a secondary status as far as shooting is concerned, and no amount of flattery about "quarterbacking" and "playmaking" and "feeding" changes the fact that in such offenses the guard is a last, desperate effort when all else fails. At Cincinnati, however, we like happy guards, and happy guards are those who participate in the scoring.

Our Five Play is designed to work the strong-side guard to a spot on the baseline halfway between the foul lane and the sideline. This play begins with our men in the Swing-and-Go positions and the ball in possession of the strong-side guard. The strong-side forward keys the play by moving outside to the extended foul line instead of swinging off the pivot man. G passes to F as soon as F reaches his new position. F passes in to the pivot man and immediately breaks toward the center to pick G's defensive man. G cuts around the outside of F and drives to his spot on the baseline, where he receives a pass from P and takes a short shot. Figure 3-12 illustrates this play and the manner in which it takes G out of a congested area into a cleared area for his shot.

There are two important points I wish to stress here. First, it is necessary for F to cut first (before G) after his pass is made in to the pivot man. G cannot break clear until F is in position to screen No. 4 defensive man out of the play. Second, F's first move is to the extended foul line, no more and no less. For some reason, the defensive man on P will invariably be caught on the wrong side when F moves to this position. I cannot explain why this happens, but it does. As a result of this lapse, our forwards are trained to keep the extended foul line in mind whenever a play calls for a pass in from forward to pivot.

While the Five Play is developing, the weak-side forward and weak-side guard must keep their defensive men occupied, either by interchanging positions or by moving opposite the ball. These two men are called our "play finishers." The weak-side forward, especially, is responsible for rebounding, and is forearmed with the knowledge of exactly where the shot will come from.

I should add, also, that we run this play from either side, on the assumption, naturally, that two happy guards are better than one.

## FAKE SCREEN

Quite often, we run into opponents whose defensive philosophy is similar to ours. They like to put pressure on right from the start, hoping to force us into mistakes. Since our offense, like all offenses, operates best against a normal defense, we must have methods for keeping the defense "honest," or in normal position.

One of our best methods is a simple little quick opener (shown in Figure 3-13). This is a fast, effective surprise play that we break off our Swing-and-Go pattern. St. Bonaventure used to use a give-and-go very similar to this quite successfully, although they used it off a different basic series.

We begin the play with a pass from the weak-side guard to the weak-side forward. The weak-side guard then breaks toward the defensive man on the strong-side guard as if to screen or pick him, then cuts abruptly down the center and takes a return pass from the weak-side forward. When executed correctly, this play has the chastening effect on the defense that we are hoping for. It seems like such an easy way to score. Actually, however, the timing of the weak-side guard has to be near-perfect to get this effect. He has to fake his screen in such a manner that the

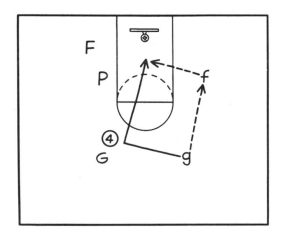

**Figure 3-13  Fake Screen.** With ball on weak side, g passes to f and then fakes screen on Number 4. g drives down center after fake and takes return pass from f.

defensive man will react by switching, yet he must not allow them time to switch. I shall attempt to explain this timing to you.

There is a vulnerable split-second, just before a switch is made, when the offensive men belong to neither defensive man. The body cannot react as quickly as the brain, of course, and though the brain orders, "Switch," the body finds itself caught in a kind of defensive vacuum as it leaves one offensive man for the other, yet is covering neither. An experienced offensive player can sense this instant. The weak-side guard must detect it and make his cut between the two closing defenders in that one fraction of time. Run in this manner, the Fake Screen can be devastating.

## THE SEVEN PLAY

Miami University of Ohio, our close neighbor to the north, came down to Cincinnati early in the 1960-61 season and gave us a terrific battle. At that time we were beginning to expand our basic patterns, and I was interested in plays that spread offensive power over the whole team, especially plays that involved scoring by the guards. I was particularly impressed by one Miami play that scored three times against us. After studying our films of the game and making the slight adjustments necessary to fit it into our own system, I borrowed the play. At practice we still call it the "Miami play," and we have used it with a good deal of success on many occasions. There ought to be some dramatic reason why we finally adopted the name Seven Play, but, if so, it escapes me. Usually we identify a play with a descriptive name that will tell the players something about its primary objective, but some names seem to evolve by themselves. So Seven Play it is, at least in public, and this is how we work it.

Coming up on offense we go into our regular Swing-and-Go positions and work the ball to the weak side. The weak-side guard passes in to the weak-side forward, then cuts inside this forward and drives for the basket, as if to take a return pass. The weak-side forward dribbles quickly to the foul line, and the strong-side guard then cuts outside him, takes a handoff, and drives in to the basket.

To work this play correctly, the strong-side guard must set up his man so he can be picked by the weak-side forward. We want this guard's defensive man to go with him so that the weak-side forward can get at least a piece of him with his pick. Meanwhile, the weak-side guard, the first to drive, continues his circle behind the strong-side forward and pivot man, and back out to his normal position.

If the defensive men on the weak-side forward and strong-side guard switch on the pick, we advise the forward to throw a delayed pass to the strong-side guard as his first option.

Notice, in Figure 3-14, that this play is keyed when the weak-side guard makes his cut inside the forward.

In running this play, as in running all plays, success depends on timing and execution. An offense is only as good as the sum of all the individual fakes, maneuvers for position, shooting accuracy, and tip-ins that make it up. In addition, offensive power increases in direct proportion to the ability of each man to take advantage of unforeseen opportunities. The man with the ball will often observe an opening in the defense that has not been charted into a particular play. He may find a clear path to the basket or a man free to take a quick pass and lay it up. When such unexpected opportunities present themselves, we

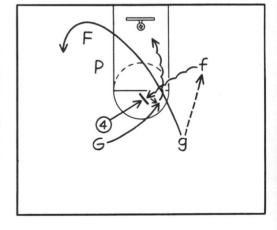

**Figure 3-14   The Seven Play.** With ball on weak side, g passes to f and cuts inside toward basket. f dribbles to foul line, hands off to G who is cutting outside f. As f partially picks or screens number 4, G drives in for the shot.

want them to be exploited. The well-planned and well-drilled plays give cohesion and organization to a pattern offense; the individual capacity for exploiting defensive mistakes gives it excitement.

## CLEARANCE PLAYS

In our Cincinnati offense we follow an unwritten rule that goes something like this: Clear out men who sag on the pivot. Since this sagging is done to clog up the area near the pivot, or to double-team him, or to prevent a pass in to him, we try to free him of extra pressure by having our guards or forwards take their men away. We leave such moves up to the individuals on the court, therefore, we cannot design set plays for clearance.

In general, we try to pass the ball to the pivot man when his defensive man has two or three personal fouls early in the game, or any time his defensive man accumulates four fouls. Since the defensive man will have to play loose, we feed the pivot man as much as possible. At such times, of course, other defensive men will try to sag on our pivot man to assist in defending him. Clearing out these helpers is mandatory.

When one of our outside men with the ball sees his pass to the pivot man result in a sag by the man guarding him, the outside man knows that he is going to get the ball back immediately from the pivot man. This return pass should be automatic and quick. In many cases this quick return pass from the pivot man defeats the sagging defensive man long enough for the outside man to get off a shot. "If you expect the ball passed in to you," we tell our pivot man, "you have to pass it outside when they're sagging." Otherwise, those boys on the outside may get a little unhappy with all that giving and no receiving.

## PIVOT SCREENS USED IN THE SWING-AND-GO SERIES

I pointed out earlier that during the running of the Swing-and-Go series the position of the strong-side forward's defensive man dictated whether the pivot man used a front pivot or a

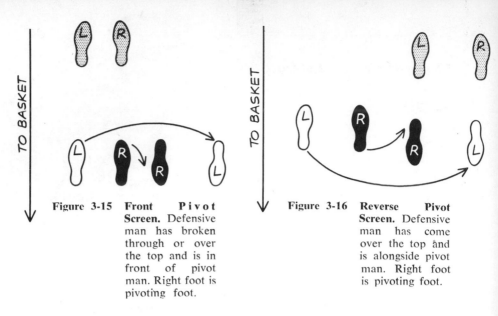

**Figure 3-15** Front Pivot Screen. Defensive man has broken through or over the top and is in front of pivot man. Right foot is pivoting foot.

**Figure 3-16** Reverse Pivot Screen. Defensive man has come over the top and is alongside pivot man. Right foot is pivoting foot.

reverse pivot to set up his screen. Since these pivots are so important to the success of the series, I want to illustrate them. In the diagrams that follow the shaded feet represent the positions of the defensive man who is to be screened, the black foot represents the pivoting foot of the pivot man, and the white foot represents his non-pivoting or sliding foot. Figures 3-15 and 3-16 show the best pivot reactions when the strong-side

**Figure 3-17** Front Pivot Screen. Pick set up by pivot man when forward goes around toward foul lane and down the center. Left foot is pivoting foot. Used when forward's defensive man is alongside pivot man.

**Figure 3-18** Reverse Pivot Screen. Pick set up by pivot man when forward goes around toward foul lane. Left foot is pivoting foot. Used when defensive man is in front of pivot man.

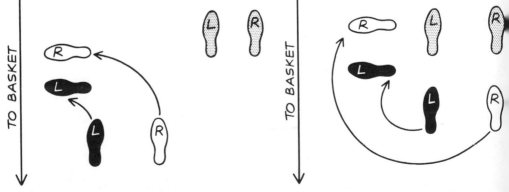

forward cuts back outside and drives for the basket, while Figures 3-17 and 3-18 show the moves to be made when the strong-side forward continues his swing around to the foul line.

To be effective, a pattern offense must consist of several distinctive series which are interchangeable. When the change is made from one series to another, however, no complicated shifting of positions should be involved. These changes are made in the heat of a ball game, remember, and this is not quite the same as making them on the practice floor or on your blackboard.

Kentucky State College is a very fortunate school. They have as their head basketball coach John McLendon, who has won championships in every single area of basketball competition. These areas include high school, college, university, amateur, international series, and professional.

In his twenty one years of coaching college basketball, Mr. McLendon has compiled an outstanding record of 477 wins against 115 losses for a percentage of .806.

# John B. McLendon, Jr.

McLendon's championship trailblazing began in 1936 when he led Lawrence Memorial High School of Lawrence, Kansas to the Kansas-Missouri Athletic Conference title.

From there, the trail led into college basketball, going first to North Carolina College at Durham, North Carolina; then to Tennessee A.&I. State University at Nashville, Tennessee, where he won the National Association of Intercollegiate Athletics championship in 1957, 1958, and 1959. He is the only coach to win three NAIA championships. He is presently coaching at Kentucky State College at Frankfort, Kentucky.

McLendon is the former coach of the Cleveland Pipers and led them to the National Industrial Basketball Championship in 1961 and the National Amateur Athletic Union Championship the same year. His Pipers were the only amateur to defeat the U.S. Olympic team. This was in 1960.

In 1961 he was named coach of the U.S.A. All-Stars who played the U.S.S.R in Russia. The outcome? U.S.A. 8 wins and 0 losses.

In 1962, McLendon was basketball specialist to South East Asia, coach of the U.S.A. All Stars who toured Russia and Europe, and the same year was inducted into Helm's Hall of Fame.

In 1964 he coached the NAIA Olympic Trails team that came in third place, and his Kentucky State College team won the Mid-West Athletic Association title.

4

# *CHAMPIONSHIP FAST BREAK*

John B. McLendon, Jr.
Basketball Coach
Kentucky State College

The term *fast break* refers to an offense which has figured strongly and significantly in the development of the game of basketball. It has been (and is now) more or less facetiously known by other names such as "firehorse," "helter-skelter," "run-and-shoot," and other such names, some complimentary, some derisive, but all referring to a kind of "running game" which demands appreciation and respect by proponents and adversaries alike.

## ADVANTAGES

I like the fast break. Frankly, I like it most because in the last 29 years of coaching high school, college, amateur, and professional basketball, it has consistently brought my teams winning seasons. However, other important technical reasons why the fast break as a primary offense is a winner are those which follow:

1. The fast break can be succesfully employed by players who have limited all-around ability, but who have one or two special abilities.

2. It can be used to offset the lack of sufficiently trained defensive personnel.

3. It can physically break down an opposing team, and in doing so, equalize or decrease the advantages held by that team.

4. The fast break offense is a good answer to the running game of the opposing team.

5. It creates the need for excellent conditioning with inclusive health practices insuring this status.

6. The fast break quickly detects those physically unready or limited.

7. It inspires the best in teamwork basketball.

8. The fast break utilizes the close shooting area and is best for consistent scoring performance.

9. It is a most versatile offense.

10. It complements more defenses than any other offense.

11. It is a winner by record, being used by more winners in all areas of basketball play than any other offense.

12. Its mechanics are simple. It is easily organized.

13. It is a high-pressure offense designed to disorganize opposing team defense and limit the opposing team's offense.

14. The fast break offense is an exciting game for the player, coach, and spectator, with great appeal to each of them. It has, by nature, the means of teaching many of life's great lessons in sportsmanship and character.

15. The fast break is basic to continued preparadness in international competition.

The theme of the fast break game is speed. It is basketball with speed added and with the offensive area of the court extended to the full length instead of the usual half court. Its main point of strength is the continuous application of speed and movement on possession of the ball toward an attack on the optimum scoring area (Figure 4-1), with offensive players out-

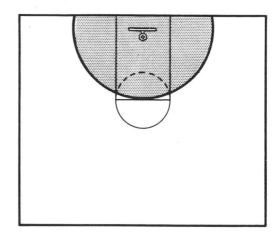

Figure 4-1 Optimum Scoring Area.

numbering the defense. The objective is to score with the high-percentage shot before the defense can numerically equalize the offense and become organized to prevent the field goal. The rush to the optimum scoring area should be initially charted through three lanes, with possible follow-up attacks through lanes four and five (Figure 4-2).

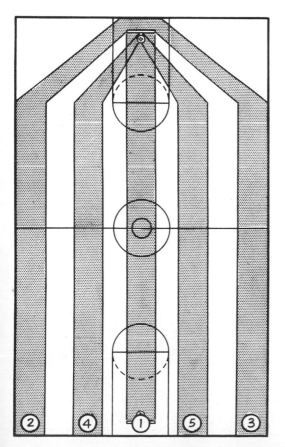

Figure 4-2 Fast Break Lanes.

## Two Fast Break Philosophies

There are many variations of the fast break attack itself, but there seem to be two main ideas on which the fast break philosophy rests and which dictate the objectives, and to a large extent, direct the mechanics of the offense.

In one idea (and, incidentally, the idea which is usually incorporated into other offensive plans) the fast break is used when the circumstances in the game allow the fast-breaking team to gain possession of the ball and to move quickly to scoring position. In this usage, the team waits for an *opportunity* to fast break. When the opportunity occurs, the fast break is on.

In the second idea (and the philosophy to which I subscribe) defensive pressure is applied to *create* situations which allow the fast break offense to operate. It is further applied from various situations on the court and continued in such a way as to cause a defensive imbalance in the back court.

When following the first idea, a team fast breaks *if it finds an opportunity to do so*. In the second idea, the team fast breaks *each time it gets possession of the ball*. In either idea there is assistance given by the defense when it uses tactics which force ball mishandling, bad passes, and other errors in play, which will enable the team to move quickly to a position of advantage. In observing a fast break team, one often sees a player break through the opposing team for a one-man drive to a field goal, or a quick, ball-hawking break through the oncoming offense to a two players versus one defender, or to a three-offense versus two-defense situation. This is a fast break objective. In fact, the ultimate objective of the fast break is to secure the numerical advantage after gaining the ball, in the *optimum scoring area* (Figure 4-1) and score. By quickly maneuvering players through speed and dynamic passing, utilizing the full court and three or more lanes of approach the offensive overload (two-on-one, three-on-one, three-on-two, etc.) is achieved. Figure 4-3 shows the overload possibilities.

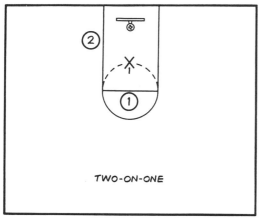

TWO-ON-ONE

**Figure 4-3   Offensive Overload Possibilities.**

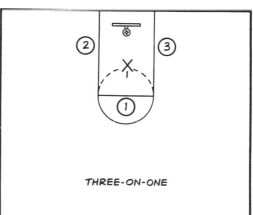

THREE-ON-ONE

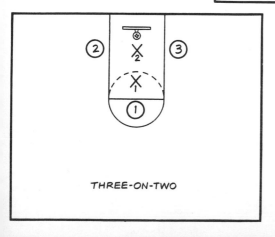

THREE-ON-TWO

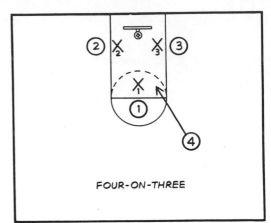

FOUR-ON-THREE

Figure 4-3 (Cont.)

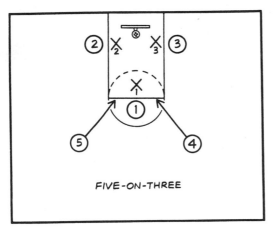

FIVE-ON-THREE

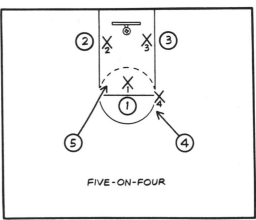

FIVE-ON-FOUR

*70*

## Beginning the Fast Break

The fast break offense is launched from certain inception points or origins. These points are at various locations on the court, depending on the phase of the game in which the team is involved or on the type and strength of defense employed. The points of fast break inception in order of their usual frequency of occurrence are:

1. Defensive rebound after a field goal missed.
2. The end line throw-in after a field goal made.
3. The end line throw-in after a free throw made.
4. The defensive rebound after a free throw missed.
5. Acquisition of the ball from the offense as it attempts to follow its plan; such as loose balls, stolen balls, interceptions, recoveries of fumbles, etc.
6. The jump ball situations.

Point 1, the defensive rebound after a field goal missed, represents the use of the fast break when the defense against it is least organized or when that defense is most vulnerable. Where Points 2, 3, 4 are concerned, the defense is more or less set, or it may have organized itself for the fast break during, or prior to, the action involved. Points noted under 5 represent (as has been indicated earlier) those inceptions resulting from defensive tactics calculated to increase the frequency of fast break scoring chances.

## Importance of Defense

An offense functions more efficiently when the defense com-

plements it. Certain offenses are better offenses if the defense
used along with it can be coordinated with the offensive objectives. To use the pressing defense with a ball-control offense,

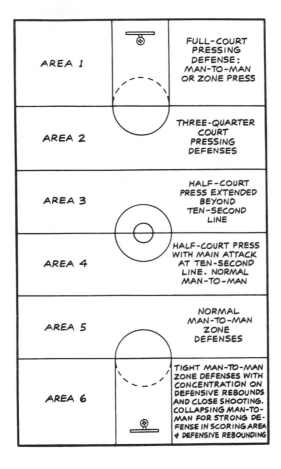

Figure 4-4   Defenses to Com-
plement the Fast
Break.

for example, would be incongruous. As far as the fast break
offense operates, the full-court pressing defense (zone or man-
to-man) is the number one complementing defense (Figure
4-4). It gives the team possession in an area where the defense
cannot recover. In terms of the areas from which the defense

can be least quickly organized, the following defenses are next in order of coordinating defense with the fast break:

Second—three-quarter court press.
Third—half-court press.
Fourth—man-to-man variations.
Fifth—three-two zone.
Sixth—two-one-two zone.
Seventh—two-three zone.

A second key to the value of a defense to fast break purposes is in the number of times a team gets possession of the ball and aligns itself in the numerical overload positions in the optimum scoring area.

To facilitate the fast break offense itself and to accomplish the purpose of overloading the defense, the players should be given certain specific responsibilities. The components of the offense and the duties of the personnel are listed below:

## THREE REBOUNDERS

There should be three rebounders—usually the center and two forwards—assigned to secure the defensive rebound regardless of the team defense employed. They must rebound (a) from a zone defense alignment and (b) from a man-to-man, block-out triangle. Any one of the three players who is engaged in rebounding has, in order of importance, the following fast break responsibilities:

1. Secure the defensive rebound.
2. Pass the outlet pass to the outlet-pass receiver.
3. Follow up the outlet pass with a fast, down-court sprint in the assigned lane. The fast break should be accom-

plished through the players filling at least three lanes; two lanes down each sideline six feet wide, one lane in the middle six feet of the court. Very often, two additional lanes are utilized (increasing the number to five) which are located halfway between the center lane and each outside lane (Figure 4-2).

4. Depending on instructions or on game strategy, the rebounders (a) follow-up rebounds on the offensive board, or (b) follow up in position for outside shooting as a "trailer," or (c) follow up in position for the close lay-up (or close shot).

Since the zone defense insures the rebound formation and other fast break alignments necesary for the fast break offense to get a flying start, that style of defense very often accompanies the fast break. The man-to-man defense, when employed properly, does more defensively than any zone can do; yet it offers a poor formation for the fast break when the field goal is attempted. However, inasmuch as my three best rebounders are going to be assigned to rebounding regardless of whether the zone or man-to-man defense is used, and the two best ball-handling dribblers are going to be assigned to receive the outlet pass and do the dribbling chore, the technique I have worked out amounts to what is a man-to-man defense and a zone rebound. This formation is assumed as the field goal attempt is made. It allows a team which is forced out of the zone, or which normally employs the man-to-man defense, to have the best of both systems, the zone for offense and the man-to-man for defense, operating to its advantage at the same time.

## THE OUTLET PASSER

One of the three rebounders is the outlet passer, who is re-

sponsible for the necessary first pass in the system. The best
passers from the rebound position can pass out right- or left-
handed after quickly determining the position of the outlet-pass
receiver.

The two forwards and the center are the players who must be
skilled in this technique. The outlet pass goes to a specified
area where a receiver (either guard) is to be waiting. In the

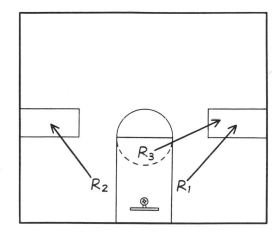

**Figure 4-5    Outlet Pass Assign-
ments.**

simplest fast break mechanics (which, incidentally, forms the
basis for the "Championship Fast Break") the rebound-
pass-out rules are as follows:

1.  Rebounds retrieved on the rebounder's left side of the
    backboard (as the rebounder faces the goal) are let out
    to the fast break team's offensive right sideline.
2.  Rebounds retrieved on the defensive rebounder's right side
    of the backboard are let out to the fast break team's
    offensive left sideline.
3.  Rebounds retrieved in the center rebound area go to the
    fast break offensive team's right sideline (Figure 4-5).

### THE RELEASED GUARD (FIRST PLAYER DOWN-COURT)

The guard opposite the outlet-pass receiving guard first breaks down-court on anticipation of his teammate securing the rebound or at the moment of possession. He follows the fast break lane opposite the side of the rebound to a position near the goal and holds there. He may, on occasions, receive a long pass for a drive-in lay-up shot, but his main function is to make the defense retreat and leave the center of the court open or defended by only one remaining guard. An appreciation of this primary function is helpful to his performance. Scoring is his secondary function.

### THE OUTLET PASS RECEIVER (THE SECOND MAN DOWN-COURT)

The outlet pass receiver is either guard. He is the opposite guard from the guard who breaks first and is the guard nearest the sideline to which the outlet pass is thrown. His position for reception varies from the corner baseline to the mid-court line six feet from the sideline, or from a position near the free-throw line extended area outward to the sideline (Figure 4-5). The actual position depends on the height, power, and skill of the outlet passers as well as, conversely, the strength of the offensive rebounders. The more powerful the offensive rebounders, the closer to the baseline the outlet-pass receiving guard positions himself. The less the strength of the offensive rebounders, the farther from the baseline and the closer to the center line the receiver can receive the ball. The optimum position to receive the outlet pass and at the same time prevent guard interference is at a point opposite the top of the free throw circle. It is to this point the guard quickly moves after briefly blocking out any offensive rebound follow-up by the opposing guard. When reaching this spot, the guard pivots and stops with his back to the sideline. From here he can see the entire court, avoid charging when dribbling, and be in a position to move toward or away from the ball, according to the action of the defensive guard or according to the pass-out freedom allowed the outlet passer.

On receiving the ball, the guard (1) immediately looks down-court for his teammate, the released guard, and throws the long pass; or (2) he dribbles to the center lane, attempting to by-pass the defender in that part of the court. He may dribble directly to the center of the court, or he may dribble the sideline a short distance and then veer toward the center and top of the circle in his goal-end of the court, from where he (3) passes off to the guard or to the player who has filled the third lane. The center lane player is usually the second player in the attack.

The best guards for the fast break are those who can dribble well and are especially effective against a single defender. The guard who can dribble past one defender, or who can control his dribble and passing in mid-court, thereby causing a two-on-one or three-on-two situation, is an invaluable asset to the fast break team. Two such guards will quicken the attack tremendously, since either can take the outlet pass and handle the middle.

## THE FAST-BREAKING REBOUNDER (THE THIRD MAN DOWN-COURT)

Each man in the fast break is important. Each must carry out his responsibility. The success of the fast break depends on each man doing his part. This is true in most team offensive ideas, but probably more so in the full court offense. Unless one of the rebounders (one center and two forwards) runs (and runs faster than his opponent), the chances of getting the essential three-on-two situation are nil. The third line must be filled by one of the three rebounders. Inasmuch as most teams manage to move two men back for fast break defense, it is my feeling (and requirement) that every fast break thrust must involve the third man. He must fill the third lane and get ahead of the ball before a third defensive man can get back *and* coordinate his defensive effort with those of his teammates in order to thwart the field goal.

Very often the outlet passer is in a position to follow his pass with a sprint to the third man assignment; otherwise, one of the two rebounders who is not in possession of the ball must accomplish this tremendously important job.

Under certain conditions, the third man may be a specifically assigned player; for instance, when his opponent is physically lacking in stamina and fails to consistently run to a defensive position, or when that offensive player is more skilled in the scoring department and has more value from this position than his fellow teammates.

To repeat, the very heart of championship fast break performance is in the ability and *determination* of one of the rebounders to break to the third lane on each occasion of ball posession before a third defensive player can retreat to a defensive position and participate in an organized defense against the three attackers. The third man's presence in the third lane, with as little as a one step advantage on the third defender, forces the defender in the middle lane (the lane down which the dribbling guard is attacking) to either retreat below the foul line or allow the ball to be passed to either of the outside drivers. The middle defender's surest defense is to play both the center and wing man until help, if any, arrives, or until the three men on attack are close to the goal where the defense will be concentrated. This situation, however, is one of those for which the offense is working.

## THE TRAILERS (THE FOURTH AND FIFTH MEN DOWN-COURT)

The two rebounders (center forwards) who fail to become a

part of the three-lane fast break are the fourth and fifth players down-court. They may be given the following assignments (Figure 4-6):

1.  Trail the three attacking players, staying in the court area near the mid-court line to defend against a possible return fast break of the opponents.

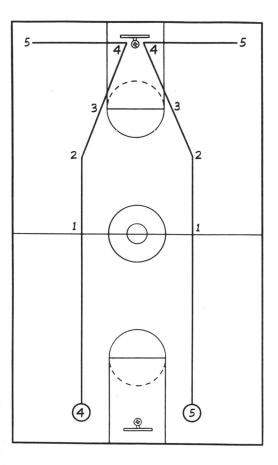

**Figure 4-6   The Trailers' Responsibility.**

2.  Trail the three players ahead to an intermediate shooting area for a center-guard pivot and pass back for the inter-

mediate field goal attempt. (This trailer usage usually calls for specific player assignment.)

3.  Fill in lane four or five, driving into the scoring area for a pass from the center-lane player or outside-lane player in what turns into a four-on-three situation.

4.  Go in strong through lane four or five for the offensive rebound after a field goal attempt (usually an assigned trailer for this job).

5.  If the fast break does not materialize to the point where a field goal attempt is considered favorable, the trailers may participate in the next phase of the offense, which may be certain free lance or pattern moves or may be simply moving quickly to the positions played in the set or half-court offense.

It should be made clear that the trailers are two of the three men who *tried* to fill the third lane, but who failed to do so because one of their number outsped them, and they thus became *forced* to play the trailer role. This, of course, may not hold true where players are specifically assigned to the third lane or trailer responsibilities. The fastest fast break is one where the personnel is versatile enough to handle any position which circumstances of play dictate.

To summarize briefly, the fast break offense, which is to be applied each time the team secures the defensive rebound, releases one guard immediately to the outside lane opposite the guard receiving the outlet pass. The guard receiving the outlet pass drives to the center of the court. All three rebounders sprint to the third lane, including the outlet passer; the first of the three rebounders to get into the third lane continues to the optimum scoring area; the two rebounders who did not get into the three-lane break move in to the defensive back-court area or into lanes 4 and 5 for the 4-on-3, 5-on-4 follow-up (Figure

4-7). When it is not advisable to make a field goal attempt, the offense, under control, moves into the set offense phase. The foregoing plan is Fast Break Plan One in my book.

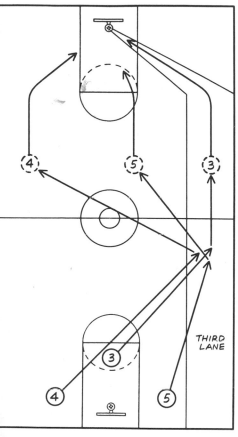

**Figure 4-7 Rebounders' Secondary Assignments.**

THIRD LANE

**Figure 4-8 A Fast Break from a Missed Free Throw.**

The fast break plan described above may be used in a similar manner, with but few adjustments, on free throw rebounds (Figure 4-8), or from an end-line thrown-in after a field goal made (Figure 4-9), or after a free throw made (Figure 4-10).

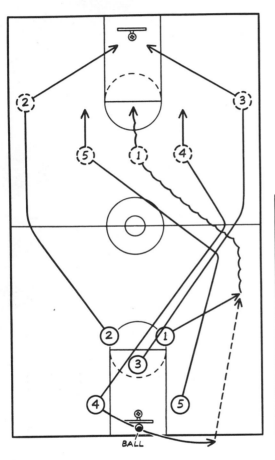

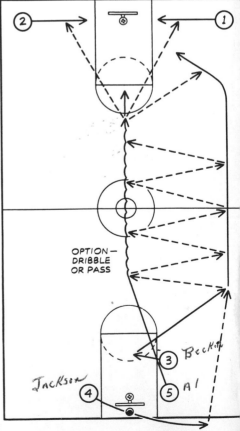

Figure 4-9   A Fast Break for Endline Throw-in after Field Goal Made.

Figure 4-10   A Fast Break Plan for Endline Thrown-in after Free Throw Made.

## "THE FREE-LANCE INTERIM PERIOD" (BETWEEN THE FAST BREAK AND THE SET OFFENSE)

The period of time between the fast break being adequately defensed and the beginning of the set offense is referred to here as the "free lance interim period," and it may be utilized in several ways. This period may be used for follow-up four-on-three or five-on-four maneuvers, which have been described under the discussion on "the trailers." Another follow-up maneuver may have the fourth or fifth man using the two cutters ahead of the ball as posts for a cut, which will free him for a high-percentage shot (Figure 4-11). Figure 4-12 shows a simple pass

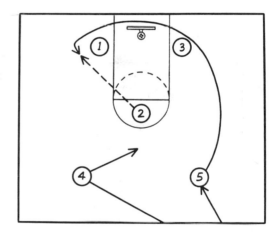

**Figure 4-11 Fast Break Trailer Scoring.**

to one outside man and a screen for the opposite outside player, who receives the ball off the screen for a close shot. The pass may go to either side. Figure 4-13 shows a pass to the outside cutter by the center-lane guard and a fake and cut behind that receiver for a short shot. This pass may go to either side also.

Needless to say, quick thinking, coordinated action in passing, and screening by the center guard are highly important in the required, fast-moving, free-lance play. If such ingredients are missing in the player personnel, the logical tactics would include

**Figure 4-12   Free-Lance    off
the Fast Break.**

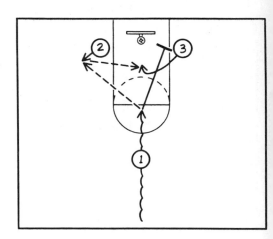

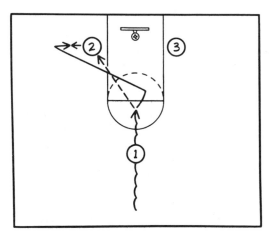

**Figure 4-13   Free-Lance    off
the Fast Break.**

"holding the ball" until the set offense formation is intact, then proceeding with the secondary offense.

VARIATIONS

The fast break offense has many variations, and a number of these plans may be employed according to the defensive reaction of the opponents. The basic plan I have used has been

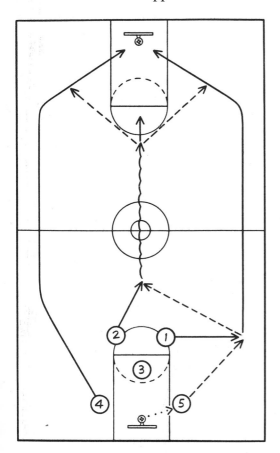

Figure 4-14   A   Fast   Break
Plan   for   the   Re-
bounder to Score.

discussed, but there are several additional plans which are used from this primary attack formation.

Plan Two (Figure 4-14) may be used for an opposing re-

bounder who does not run well, or who will not run. The
rebounder in this plan is the number one man down court. The
additional value of this plan is evident when one of the back
court defenders picks this man up and has to keep him as the
set offense is employed. The defender in such cases is usually
physically overmatched.

   Plan Three (Figure 4-15) is an exceptionally fast, fast break,
based on the ability of one of the rebounders being able to man
the center lane.

**Figure 4-15  A  Fast  Break
Plan  for  a  Re-
bounder  in  the
Center Lane.**

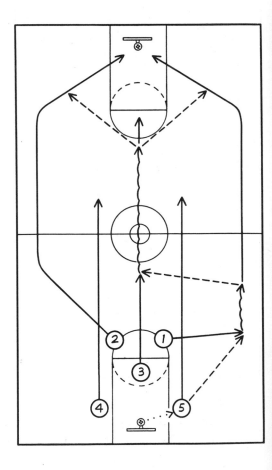

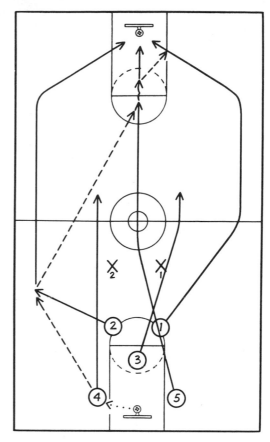

**Figure 4-16 A Fast Break Plan for the Big Man Down Center.**

Plan Four (Figure 4-16) is designed for the big man down center. It has similar advantages to Plan Two.

### FAST BREAK PRINCIPLES

Regardless of the plan used, the following principles and suggestions must be observed in the development of the fast break offense:

1.  There must be a thorough grounding in fundamentals of ball handling, passing, dribbling, pivoting, rebounding, and lay-up shooting, with extra emphasis on speed in execution.

87

2. The team must be conditioned to a point of physical superiority.

3. "Fast Break" must be the first thought and action in all situations. There is a plan for every game circumstance. It must be attempted and forced on the opposition, if possible.

4. A complementing defense must be coordinated with the fast break offense in order to increase the possibilities of ball possession and subsequent scoring. The best defense in this category is the pressing defense.

5. A fast-dribbling, strong guard with passing dexterity who can control the center lane attack represents an all-important player, whose development requires arduous work, but which is well worth all the time and effort spent.

6. The players must believe that as personnel of a fast break team, they are unique in terms of conditioning, determination, and dedication to the hard game they are playing.

7. The coach must believe in the full-court, fast-breaking game as a primary offense.

8. The fast-breaking game usually is the game you can best influence the opponents to play.

All coaches will use the fast break if the opportunity occurs; I believe that opportunity can be created practically every time you get the ball.

One of the most successful basketball
coaches in the country is Eddie Hickey, the
former coach at Marquette University.
Hickey, who entered the coaching field in 1926, has held posts at Creighton high school, Creighton University, St. Louis University, and Marquette.

He was named head basketball coach at Creighton University in 1935
and promptly led the Bluejays to a share of the Missouri Valley conference title. Creighton won two more conference championships outright
and shared another title under Hickey. It also played in the National

# Eddie Hickey

Invitational Tournament twice and the NCAA once before Hickey departed for St. Louis in 1947.

Hickey left Creighton with a fine record of 132 victories and only 72 losses, but he was to have even greater success at St. Louis.

In his first year at the helm, St. Louis won 24 of 27 games and captured the NIT title. In his 11 years at St. Louis, Hickey sent 6 teams to the NIT. The "Bills" also made two trips to the NCAA under Hickey's tutelage, won the Sugar Bowl tournament twice and the Cotton Bowl championship once. Hickey left St. Louis with a mark of 212 victories and 89 defeats.

Hickey was named Missouri Valley Conference "Coach of the Year" in both 1952 and 1957, and the Basketball Writers' Association selected him as "Coach of the Year" following the 1958-59 season, when Marquette ranked among the nation's top teams and posted a 23-6 record.

# 5

# *INDIVIDUAL AND TEAM DEFENSE*

Eddie Hickey
Basketball Coach (Ret.)
Marquette University

## WHY DEFENSE IS IMPORTANT

Emphasis on individual and team defense is increasing rapidly. This is especially true because there has been so much of an increase in the offensive ability of the youngsters coming up. Boys score better now than ever in the history of the game, and it is extremely important that defense make progress and keep stride. Otherwise, the game of basketball will become overbalanced.

Not everyone has the same ability in touch, perception, in judgement of space and distance that makes a good offensive player and scorer. But a player can be pretty constant in his activity in playing defense with some physical qualifications. His defensive ability will hold him up when it would otherwise be impossible for him to play because of an inability to score.

A basket saved is just as good as one made. That is the whole principle in emphasizing defense. Most of the time, keeping the opposing player from scoring will lead to desperation moves, which, in turn, will lead to mistakes. If a boy can force a mistake on defense and then capitalize on it, he will become, in effect, a better offensive player.

I feel that the player who can't be an asset to the team on offense will make up for it with scrap and hustle on defense. This is particularly true in the younger boy who has not matured fully and doesn't have all his strength or agility. He can't snap the ball from player to player because he doesn't have that quickness in his ball-handling movements. But he can still be a great factor on his team because of his ruggedness and toughness on defense.

### INDIVIDUAL DEFENSE

The old masters of the days gone by have taught us that there are certain factors of defensive play that we might refer to as "fundamentals of defense." These are: (1) Position, (2) Stance, (3) Footwork, (4) Aggressiveness, (5) Physical Condition, (6) Pride.

### DEFENSIVE POSITIONING

Positioning is definitely the beginning of all defensive play, whether it is on a team or individual basis. Ordinarily, we want our defensive man to be between his man and the basket. This is what we call the orthodox position. However, there are some areas on the court where the defensive player would vary that position. Under some circumstances, he would be playing in front of his man, and under others, he might be playing at his side.

I definitely feel the defense should be unorthodox against the single post. The defensive man will be playing in front and to the side of this man as much as he will be playing between him and the basket. This makes it difficult for the pivot man to receive the ball unless he moves beyond his normal area of play. You will be making him operate where his timing will be off and where he won't be quite so effective.

Another example of an unorthodox defensive position would be against the corner man. Overplaying this side man to keep him from getting possession of the ball is often done. Some ball clubs start most of their offensive patterns by passing to one particular corner man. Keeping this man from getting the ball reduces the effectiveness of the entire offensive attack.

Finally, if the press is on down-court, then the baseline players will definitely have to be played in an unorthodox manner to prevent them from receiving the ball.

The above exceptions to the rule prove that positioning is something you just can't tie down. You must bring it into focus with the team's overall objectives.

## STANCE

Stance is the positioning of the entire body from the tips of the toes right up to the tips of the fingers. The preferred stance is a slightly staggered one with one foot slightly in front of the other. It is mandatory that one foot be advanced, especially when playing against the ball.

We advocate that the knees be bent so the player can get into action quickly. If the muscles are not flexed, the boy is going to be left behind. As an example, boys lining up for the 100-yard dash aren't all erect. Since they want to take off and get quick movement, they get down with their hands to the ground ready to go.

We can't get that low in basketball; but it must be understood that if we are to have this unfolding of muscular control in explosive movement, we must first have the flexion and extension of muscles. With the knees bent, they can be straightened out and movement can be initiated.

There must be a coordination of muscular movement on defense. Therefore, if your right foot is forward, your right hand should be up. However, I do not advocate that old hue and cry,

"Keep your hands up—keep your hands up." You don't play good defense running around the court with your hands waving.

I think the hands should be carried rather low and should be reaching out and coming up from the floor. Of course, when the ball is involved, you want that hand raised with the ball. The biggest mistake most boys make in this is to get their hand up and not out. We want the hand stretched toward the ball and not just extended straight up. If you can't get to the ball, this movement will at least offer some obstruction to your opponent's vision and hamper his concentration on making his shot.

My feeling on the stance and use of the hands might best be illustrated by the leopard in the jungle stalking his dinner. He is crouched, his muscles are tense, and he is ready to spring at the first opportunity. At the moment of decision, his paw is up, delivering the fatal blow. This could be likened to guarding a man—hands down until he receives the ball, and then a quick extension of the hand ready to block the ball.

### FOOTWORK

I prefer a staggered stance with one foot or the other advanced. This is a very controversial issue among coaches, and I think the foot position should depend a great deal upon the overall type of play and upon just where you want to control your opponent's attack. You might want to turn them inside or perhaps to the sidelines.

Ordinarily, I prefer the inside foot advanced. By inside, I mean the foot closer to the middle of the court. Most coaches feel they are a little stronger toward the open side—the side where the player's rear foot is located. They feel that by concentrating the weakness of the individual stance itself toward the middle of the court, they are actually making the overall team defense stronger. By sinking or sluffing off, your players can help each other when the ball is forced to the middle. We tell our players that the officials are not going to allow us to have one of our men sitting in the front row on the sidelines to help us on defense; but by turning the ball back toward the middle, they can get some help from their teammates.

However, when defensing the baseline, we like to change our foot positions. Since we want to cut the baseline off, we will have our outside foot forward. This goes back to the same principle of forcing the ball to an area where you can receive assistance from your teammates.

## GUARDING THE MAN WITH THE BALL

We prefer that our defensive players keep their hands low and slap up at the ball rather than slap down. There are many variables that would determine how close your defensive man would play to his opponents. A tall man wouldn't play as close as a short man. A slow defensive man can't play too close or he will lose his man. Other determining factors would be the offensive man's ability to dribble and drive, and his outside shooting ability.

If the offensive man dribbles to the open side, have your defensive player just slide with him and use the hand closest to the ball to slap up. If the man on offense wants to iron over and go the other way, the defensive player simply pivots and slides and goes at the ball with the opposite hand.

Some coaches tell their boys to watch the hands of the opponents—others say watch the feet. I tell my boys to get an overall picture but watch the belt buckle. Regardless of how much faking he does, that belt buckle is going with him. This is an important point as far as the focus of your eyes is concerned. It should be right at the middle of your opponent's body.

## GUARDING THE MAN WITHOUT THE BALL

Many of the points listed above hold true while guarding the man without the ball. Perhaps you would not have your defensive player play his man as tightly if he did not have the ball. This, of course, would depend upon his closeness to the basket.

It is extremely difficult to guard an outstanding player, especially when he receives the ball near the basket. This is why I feel that one of the most important ways of "stopping" the opposing star is to keep him from getting the ball. Again, this depends upon how close he plays to the basket area. If he lines up away from the basket area, the defense won't be as concerned about keeping the ball from him. Of course, all of the defensive principles enter into keeping a man from getting the ball. Your defensive player will be playing his man tightly and will be trying to prevent this man from receiving the pass with defensive faking. I think this is the key to keeping the ball away from any offensive man. The defensive player doesn't try to intercept the ball—he just wants to keep his man from getting it himself. If he tries to steal the ball, he most likely will overcommit himself and be faked out of position. In all probability, this will result in a basket for your opposition.

## STOPPING THE JUMP SHOOTER

The jump shot is almost impossible to stop in today's game. Your first principle of defense has got to be: "Stop the jumper from receiving the ball in his high-percentage shooting area." This principle lends great strength to the aggressiveness of your defense. It involves overplaying, challenging, and not letting the ball be received.

Of course, after they get the ball there is not much you can do except jump with them. This is contrary to most of the old-timers' thinking about defense. The old story was that you never left your feet until you could see daylight between the ball and the man shooting it.

I think when there is a certainty of the offense making the jump, there has to be the defensive jump with a full extension of the hands. This would necessitate an extended arch which would be unnatural for the shooter. If we can't block the shot we at least want a hand in the face of the shooter. We want to force him to hurry his shot. We want him to shoot off-balanced because he has to shoot so quickly.

Some coaches teach their boys to aim their block at the shooter's arm or wrist—thus throwing the shot off. Others advocate bumping the shooter as he goes up for his shot. This, too, throws the shot off. These are illegal tactics, however, and there is no place in basketball for anyone teaching these tactics.

## DESIRE AND DEDICATION

To be an outstanding player, you must have desire and be dedicated to the game. This is particularly true in proportion to the lack of physique. There can be an addition to the opportunity to play because of a greater proportion of heart, desire, and dedication to effort. As a matter of fact, we college coaches look very hard for these attributes when we are recruiting. We want to recruit the boys who are willing to sacrifice. They must be dedicated to the game and have plenty of heart.

Many boys become good defensive players simply through hard work and aggressiveness. Of course, the boy must be in good condition. He must have pride and enjoy the fact that he saves points for his team, even though it isn't registered in the scorebook. The thing I enjoy most about good defensive play is that almost anyone can become a good defensive player. It just takes hard work.

## Team Defense

### TALKING ON DEFENSE

Communication by the boys on defense is a requirement. You just can't have team defense if there isn't a combination of effort that is created by contact with each other. Teammates can give each other encouragement by talking.

Key words on defense are: *stay*—keeping same opponent; *switch*—trading opponents; *back*—returning instantly to immediate former coverage (used against a change of direction); *challenge*—advance to set defense at "point" of ball (must be used to kill dribble in a dribbling fast break.); *Ball*—used any time ball is loose or fumbled; *Board*—used any time shot goes over you to indicate board play for your teammates.

As I have said, talking on defense is mandatory for my players. To give an example, let's use the word *board*. I tell my boys that if they don't say "board," I will give them the board by letting them come over and sit with me on the bench.

### SWITCHING

Despite what some coaches say, I don't think there is a coach alive who doesn't actually advocate that there be a change of men in some instances. It is a physical impossibility not to switch with all the movement that goes on out there on the basketball floor. It's ridiculous to assume that a boy can't be trapped or doesn't need help from his teammates at times. There isn't a boy playing basketball today who can cope with team play without having to have help from his teammates at some time. As a matter of fact, it just isn't good defensive basketball not to switch at times. When an error in position, an error in play, or a lack of balance slows a boy up and his man is loose, it doesn't make sense if somebody doesn't cover him.

Of course, this is a pretty tricky situation. If, on the other hand, you have a completely free-switching game, you are pretty much at the mercy of your players. They will give you the excuse, "Well, it wasn't my man, coach, I switched." So you want to arrive at a happy medium. Switching is a team development, and the choice to switch or not to switch depends upon the situation and what the opponents are doing with the ball.

Generally speaking, I have the man nearest the baseline call the switch. Of course, he calls "pick, pick, pick" as soon as he sees his man setting a pick on a teammate. If he sees that this vocal signal has helped his teammate so that the teammate can beat the pick, he would call "stay." The teammate would know to stay with his man. If he sees that the teammate is trapped, he would call "switch" and then they would exchange men.

The exception to this general rule would be in the case of lateral movements. In this situation neither would be closer to the baseline. I think this is a coordinating effort, and the more experienced boy will call stay or switch in this situation. I think that this is the ideal situation—to have the old head on the team, the more experienced boy, making the call. This will enable the older players to more or less lead and direct the younger players. So, I think that there has to be some latitude for the talk occurring. This would depend not only on the men in the more favorable position on defense but also on the man with the more dominant personality.

Of course, there are several things to be considered concerning switching, just as there are things to be considered in determining your actions for any phase of the game. For example, you might want to play a retreating defense against a particular team. This would allow for plenty of switching and might fool your opponents into thinking that you are playing a zone. This retreating, switching defense will help your rebounding because it leaves your big men near the basket area. This, in turn, helps your fast break offense. So your decision whether to switch or not will result from a blending of all your ideas of offense and defense.

### SAGGING DEFENSE

I believe in "cheating a little" on defense in one respect. I will have any defensive players who are farthest from the ball drop off their man in order to help where the most action is. For example, if the ball is in possession of the offensive guard or forward on the left side of the floor, then I will have my defensive forward on the opposite side of the floor drop back toward the baseline so that he can help out if needed. In this way, he can watch the movement of the ball and his opponent without turning his head.

Another illustration of this principle concerns the defensive play of the guards. If the left offensive guard has the ball, then I have my right defensive guard drop back from his man and play in front of the center to keep him from receiving the pass. If the guard with the ball passes to the unattended offensive guard, then the defensive guard comes back out and covers him, and the other defensive guard drops back to take his place. This is an especially effective move if you are playing a team with a high-scoring pivot man or a team which passes to the pivot a lot to start their patterns.

### OVERPLAYING

Most basketball players have set offensive moves that they use over and over. Most left-handed dribblers will go only to the left and right-handed dribblers only to the right. If we discover through our scouting reports that a future opponent has a player or two who can go only to one particular side, then we will "overplay" this player to his strong side. This is to say that we will shift to his strongest side and practically invite this boy to try to dribble the opposite way. Depending on his ability to reverse and go to his weak side, we may play him left shoulder to left shoulder or even as much as a full step to the left or as little as just slightly to his strong side. In any event, I want my defensive players continually forcing their opponents into going to their weakest side with the ball.

## ADVANTAGE OF PLAYING A MAN-TO-MAN DEFENSE

The immediate advantage, of course, is the physical development of the players. If you are not playing a man-to-man and someone is going to help each player do his job all the time, there won't be the individual challenge for this player to develop his ability and skill. This player knows that someone will help him out if he loses his man. Of course, I believe in a help-out defense, but there has to be pride built in your players that they can do the job themselves.

By playing a man-to-man, the coach can do a good job as far as match-ups are concerned. That is, he can assign his best defensive player to the "star" of the opposing team. He can assign his big men to guard their big men. His small, quick guards can concentrate on the small, quick guards of the opposition.

Some coaches say a team fouls more when playing man-to-man. While it is true you might decide to go to a zone to protect one of your players in foul trouble, I can answer that statement in one sentence. I don't think a boy can be a good basketball player if he doesn't foul, because you have to be aggressive to play defense and the aggressiveness will create situations where the player will foul unintentionally.

## DISADVANTAGE OF PLAYING A MAN-TO-MAN DEFENSE

The biggest deterrent as far as playing a man-to-man is concerned, is that you leave yourself susceptible to being controlled by your opponent. If you assign a player to guard a particular man, he must cover that man no matter where he goes on the court. This means that he is going to have to change positions. What that man does will motivate your player in his actions. He won't be fulfilling his basic assignment if he doesn't cover him. If you don't scout your opponents and devise ways to combat the control their offense will have on your defense, you will be in for a hectic night.

Ray Mears came to the University of Tennessee in 1962 after establishing a fantastic winning record at small Wittenberg College in Springfield, Ohio. His achievements included capturing the NCAA college division championship in 1961 and an overall record of 121 victories against 23 losses in six years of collegiate coaching.

The following season, despite having to start from scratch after losing all but one of his starters, Mears guided his team to the quarter finals of the NCAA tournament.

# Ray Mears

Many professional honors have been bestowed upon him, including coach of the year in Ohio collegiate circles.

Under Mears' tutelage, Wittenberg for three seasons used its tough zone defense to hold its opponents to the lowest scoring totals of any team in the nation. On offense, Mears' teams play a disciplined game, working for the good shots that assure a high field-goal percentage.

Since coming to Tennessee, Mears has lifted the fortunes of the "Vols" so greatly that they are constantly contenders for the Southeastern Conference title.

6

# TENNESSEE'S ZONE AND COMBINATION DEFENSE

Ray Mears
Basketball Coach
University of Tennessee

About 85 percent of the college coaches in the United States have the same basic philosophy in regard to basketball. I consider myself one of the remaining 15 percent. I have always felt that the unorthodox method of coaching, while controversial, is the most stimulating and successful.

All coaches agree that a zone defense has a place in basketball, but they don't regard it as a team's basic defense. I have heard many coaches say that a zone defensive team couldn't win a state championship or any major college tournament. Statements of that nature always have been a challenge to me.

### ADVANTAGES OF PLAYING A TOUGH ZONE DEFENSE

1. It forces the opponents to play a different game than one they want to play.
2. It takes more time to penetrate a zone defense; therefore, it is an ideal defense for a team using a deliberate offense. It helps to control the tempo of the game.
3. It enables the coach to use tall personnel more efficiently because he can keep them inside.

4. Its compactness weakens a driving team or one that likes eastern style give-and-go basketball.
5. It is a good defense from which to execute a fast break.
6. It affords a player an opportunity to use his own judgment on various maneuvers. He is given the liberty to intercept a pass or double team a man if he so desires.
7. It will reduce the number of personal fouls. Also, you can switch a player from one area of the zone to another when he is in foul trouble without seriously hurting the team defense.
8. It is an excellent defense to use when you have very little or no pre-game information on your opponent.

### DISADVANTAGES OF PLAYING A TOUGH ZONE DEFENSE

1. Contrary to the belief of many coaches, it doesn't conserve energy. Everybody moves with the ball in a zone. Only the man guarding the man with the ball and the men guarding the cutters move when playing a man-to-man defense.
2. It requires excellent teamwork and constant, intelligent chatter. This only comes after hours of constant drilling.
3. There are times when one man must defense two men.
4. It is difficult to handle a team with exceptional outside shooters.
5. It requires well-conditioned men who will hustle downcourt more rapidly on defense than on offense. The defense must be set before the offensive men reach the top of the foul circle. Once the offense penetrates the defense, the zone defense is weakened.

### THE VERSATILE 1-2-2 ZONE DEFENSE

1. Figure 6-1: This is the defensive alignment used to meet the initial offensive attack. X-1 is our fastest man and in

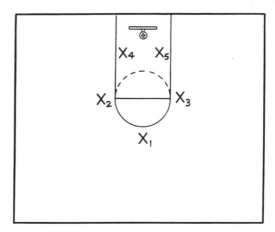

**Figure 6-1  1-2-2  Zone  De-fense.**

most cases is a guard. X-2 is our other guard and X-3 is our fastest forward. X-4 is our other forward and X-5 is our pivot man. X-1 takes a position on top of the foul circle. He may move out two to three paces depending upon the outside shooting ability of the opponents. X-3 and X-2 take a position about two feet outside the foul circle at a point in direct line with the foul line. X-4 and X-5 take a position four to five feet in front of the basket and two feet from the side of the foul line. The starting position of the defensive man varies with the alignment of the offense.

2. Figure 6-2: This shows the defensive alignment when the ball is at a right wing position. X-1 drops back to a posi-

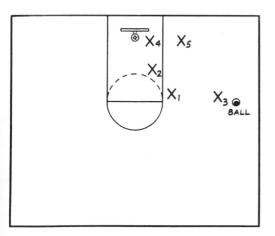

**Figure 6-2  Alignment  When Ball  Is  in  Right-Wing  Position.**

tion opposite the foul line. X-1 usually plays in front of the offensive man playing the high post position. X-3 plays the man with the ball tough and tries to prevent the sideline drive. X-2 takes a position inside the foul lane and at a spot between the ball and the corner opposite the ball. X-5's position is approximately four feet outside the foul lane. If there is an offensive man in the corner, X-5 will take a position closer to the corner. X-4 moves the same direction as X-5 and maintains the same distance between X-5. It is a good idea to visualize having an 8-foot rope tied between X-4 and X-5. Whatever direction one moves, the other must move that same direction.

3. Figure 6-3: This shows the defensive alignment when the ball is in the right corner. X-1 penetrates to a position to the right of the foul line and 4 feet in front of the 15-foot

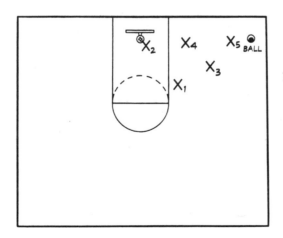

Figure 6-3    Alignment    When Ball   Is   in   Right Corner.

foul line. X-3 drops back to a position on the floor, 4 feet in front of X-5 and about 8 feet from the baseline. X-3 is in an excellent position to prevent the man with the ball from driving to his left or inside the zone defense.

X-5 plays the man with the ball tough and takes a position that would prevent a baseline drive. X-4 moves to a position directly in line with X-5, and the distance between them remains the same as before the shift. X-4 has orders to stop the man with the ball if he defeats X-5 and drives the baseline. X-2 takes a position in a straight line with X-4 and X-5 and 2 feet behind the basket.

4. The slides covered in the previous material are generally accepted 1-2-2 zone slides. We like to vary our defensive maneuvers. Our philosophy is that changing defensive slides confuse the offense. A good example of this is when the right offensive wing passes the ball to the right offensive corner man. We cover this maneuver three different ways. They arc:

a. The basic 1-2-2 zone slide that was previously explained (See Figure 6-3.)

b. X-3 slides into the corner, X-1 slides into the right defensive wing position and X-2 slides into the inside defensive front position. This is shown in Figures 6-4a and 6-4b. We slide X-3 to the corner rather

**Figures 6-4a and 6-4b   Variation #1—When Ball Is in Right Corner.**

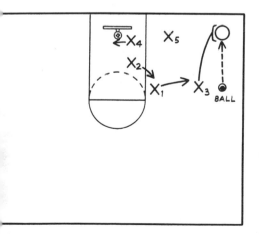 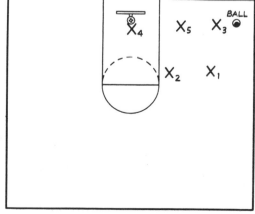

than X-5 if the offensive corner man is a weak
shooter. We want to encourage the poor shooter to
take more than his share of the shots, so by sliding
X-3 to the corner, we are actually giving him a few
seconds to get his shot off. This keeps him from
passing the ball to a teammate who is in a better
position to shoot.

c. X-1 slides into the corner, X-1 slides into the
middle spot of the three back-line defensive positions, and X-2 slides into the inside, defensive front
position. This is shown in Figures 6-5a and 6-5b.
This is a great maneuver when you have a tall X-1
man. This is another way of covering the ball in the
corner, in addition to the basic slides and the slides
in Figures 6-4a and 6-4b. This can be done only if
X-1 is a big guard. The reason for performing this
movement is to: (1) leave X-4 in better rebound
position; (2) obtain the advantages of X-1's quickness between the ball and the basket.

5. We have three ways of defensing the ball when the offense
has penetrated into a corner off a pass. They are:

a. As previously discussed when explaining the tradi-
tional 1-2-2 zone slides.

b. A double-team offensive maneuver as shown in
Figures 6-6a and 6-6b. We feel that a corner position is the weak offensive maneuvering area. X-5
and X-3 will double team the ball. X-1 moves to the
near sideline to cut the direct passing lane from the
corner position. X-2 moves from the underneath
position to the inside front position that was vacated
by X-1. Naturally, the baseline area opposite the
basket is weak. X-3 uses his own judgement when

to double team. X-3 keys his teammates. He can call a number or a name to let his teammates know the two-man trap or double team is on. X-1 will play between the ball and the man next to the ball. X-5 and X-3 guard their men high to prevent the lob pass. If the offensive man gets the ball out, we prefer him to bounce pass.

**Figures 6-5a and 6-5b   Variation #2—When Ball Is in Right Corner.**

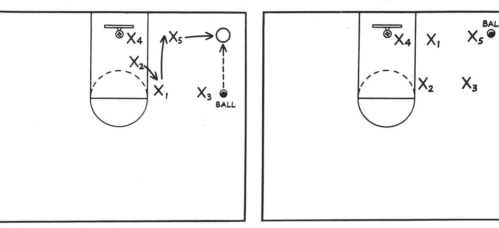

**Figures 6-6a and 6-6b   Double-Team Maneuver.**

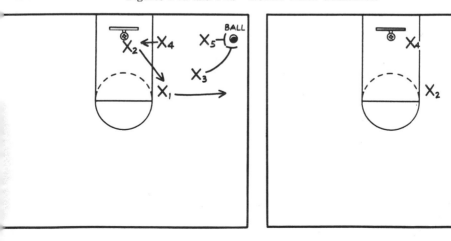

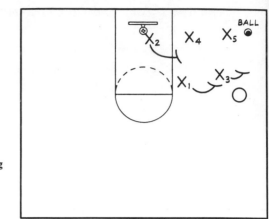

Figure 6-7a Ball-Stealing
Maneuver.

c. A maneuver designed to steal the ball as shown in Figure 6-7a and 6-7b. X-3 moves between corner offensive man and right offensive wing man. X-1 positions himself in the inside front position so he can try to intercept a long pass to a front man or pick off a pass in the high post area. We use this in two instances: (1) when the man in the corner with the ball is a big guy who isn't too agile (2) when the man in the corner has stopped his dribble and is dead.

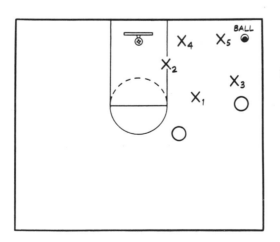

Figure 6-7b Ball-Stealing
Maneuver.

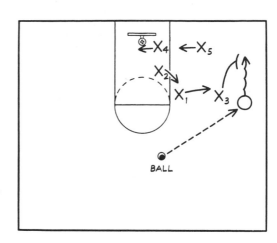

Figure 6-8a   Man-to-Man
Coverage on a
Baseline Drive.

6. We like to use man-to-man coverage on a baseline drive from the offensive wing position as shown in Figures 6-8a and 6-8b.

   a. When wing man has possession of the ball, X-3 gives him a tight, overbalanced to baseline side, man-to-man defense.

   b. X-3 tries to prevent the set and the baseline drive. If X-3 decides to drive toward the foul circle or key-hole, X-1 is responsible for controlling that maneuver.

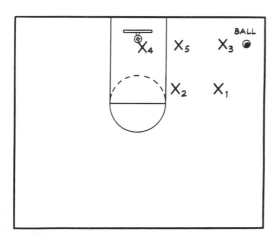

Figure 6-8b   Man-to-Man
Coverage on a
Baseline Drive.

117

c. If the wing man drives toward the baseline, X-3 disregards the zone rules and plays the offensive man a tight man-to-man defense as shown in Figure 6-8a.

d. X-1 slides to the outside front position as X-2 moves into the inside front position.

e. If X-3 is successful in containing the dribbler, he will force him into the corner and the zone coverage will be the usual 2-3 as shown in Figure 6-8b.

7. We use matching zone coverage.

a. We will try to match the defensive men with the offensive alignment, and still use the zone principle. This isn't an automatic maneuver. Normally we stay with our basic 1-2-2 zone until we see we are getting scored upon consistently. When a coach chooses to use a 1-3-1 offense, we may counter with a 1-3-1 zone defense. We do this when the offensive high post man scores consistently. Figure 6-9 will show how we move into a 1-3-1 zone defense when the offense breaks a man into the high post area. The defensive man on the side where the offensive man

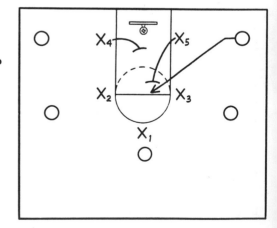

**Figure 6-9  Shift from 1-2-2 to 1-3-1 Defense.**

moves into the high post becomes the middle man
on defense. As shown in Figure 6-9, X-5 breaks
into the high post area with the offensive cutter, and
X-4 slides underneath.

b. The offensive alignment that makes it tough on X-1
is the 2-3 zone or the 2-1-2 zone. X-1 must play
both men, and if the team has two outstanding offensive guards, they will eventually free a man for the

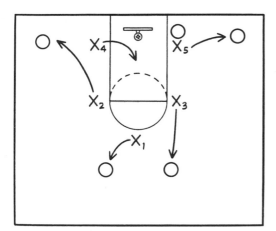 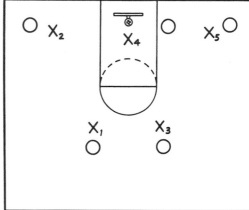

**Figures 6-10a and 6-10b—Shift from 1-2-2 to 2-3 Defense.**

long jump shot. This is a situation that will force
us to rotate out of our basic 1-2-2 zone into a 2-3
zone. We use a clockwise defensive rotation as
shown in Figures 6-10a and 6-10b. X-4 is the big
man instead of X-5. X-4 will be our big defensive
pivot, and the rotation will strategically place him
in the middle position of the defensive back line.
Figure 6-10a shows how each defensive man rotates
clockwise on the signal by X-1. Once we make the
rotation, we play a straight 2-3 or 2-1-2 zone defense.

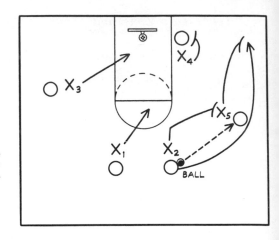

**Figure 6-11  Combination #1.**
Guard passes to
side and cuts out-
side.

8.  Combination Situations.

    a.  If the man with the ball passes to the side and runs
        to the corner, X-5 picks him up and X-2 takes X-5's
        man. This is a man-to-man defense, but we want the
        offense to think we are still in a zone. (Figure 6-11)

    b.  No matter if the guard cuts through the inside or the
        outside of the man with the ball, we still switch as
        in Figure 6-11. Up to that point, we are giving man-
        to-man coverage. At that point we will move back
        to our zone coverage. (Figure 6-12)

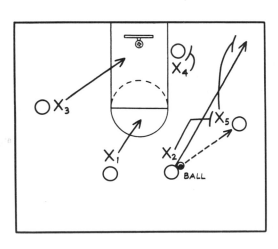

**Figure 6-12  Combination #2.**
Guard passes to
side and cuts in-
side.

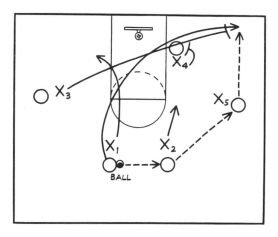

Figure 6-13 Combination #3. Weak-side guard drives through to corner.

c. If the weak-side guard moves to the corner in the above situation, X-3 covers him and X-1 covers X-3's position (Figure 6-13). From then on, it is the same as the coverage in Figure 6-12.

d. If the strong-side guard goes straight down the middle and then to the corner, we have X-3 cover him and X-1 cover X-3's position (Figure 6-14). Then the coverage will be the same as in Figure 6-13.

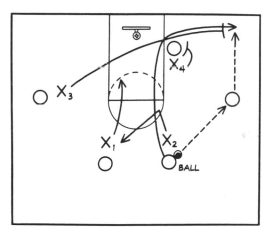

Figure 6-14 Combination #4. Strong-side guard goes through middle to corner.

121

e. On occasion, when the weak-side forward runs through, we will have X-1 drop back to cover him,

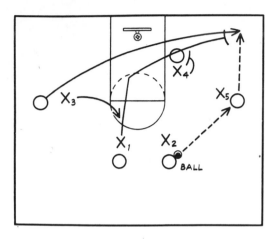

**Figure 6-15   Combination #5.**
Weak-side for-
ward goes
through to corner.

and X-3 covers X-1's area (Figure 6-15). X-3 will have to call "corner." Then X-1 will know to go to the corner.

Since Ben Carnevale became head coach
in 1946, the United States Naval Academy
has never had a losing season. Ben's first
Navy team won 16 of 17 games and an invitation to the NCAA tournament, the Middies' first such appearance. Ben was accorded honors as
"Collegiate Coach of the Year" and mentor of the Eastern College All-
Stars. His Eastern stars topped a Western aggregation in the annual
classic.

Since 1947, Carnevale has led Navy to five more post-season tournament appearances, four in the NCAA tourney and one in the National

# Ben Carnevale

Invitation Tournament since. The Middies twice advanced to the second round of the National Collegiate Tournament. His 1961-62 team played Duquesne in the NIT.

Before going to the Naval Academy, Carnevale was head coach at the University of North Carolina for two years. While there, his teams won the Southern Conference title twice and the Eastern NCAA title in 1946. His two-year record at North Carolina was 51-11.

A tireless worker, Ben is respected in his profession as one of the finest collegiate coaches. His Navy teams are noted for their basketball soundness and defensive prowess. Carnevale is a popular choice for high school and college coaching clinics and as an after-dinner speaker. He has conducted clinics in Europe for the State Department and the Armed Forces.

# 7

# *PRESSING DEFENSES*

Ben Carnevale
Basketball Coach
U. S. Naval Academy

One of the best defensive weapons a team can possess is the ability to apply a press effectively. I feel that pressing defenses are the coming thing in basketball, and I think that in a few years most teams will be using some sort of pressing defense.

## WHY PRESS?

There are many factors involved when considering whether or not to press, and the coach has to decide when to use it and when to call it off. The coach knows his team's capabilities and limitations better than anyone else. If a team doesn't have depth, the coach might decide not to press, since you are more foul-prone while pressing.

If his team doesn't have speed or quick reactions, it would be foolish for him to press. On the other hand, maybe he can successfully press one team and is unsuccessful with the next team because they are quicker, better ball-handlers, or their particular attack overcomes his press. Consequently, I think he must analyze every team he faces. The coach must decide whether his press will hurt that particular ball club or whether their attack is good enough to make his using the press foolish.

There are many conditions that warrant the use of a press. It could be as a surprise element against a slow team or a poor ball-handling team. You may want to press a team that has a good big man in the pivot to force them to commit their offense prior to their getting down in their offensive territory. You may decide to press a team with weak guards or a team whose outlet passers are poor ball-handlers. You may decide to press a young, inexperienced ball club, or you might decide to press the slow, deliberate ball club in order to speed up the game.

One big thing to consider is the fear aspect. Many coaches fear a press, and they subconsciously pass this fear on to their players. Such a ball club has two strikes against it before you even start your press against them.

### Don't Try To Steal the Ball

My basic philosophy is that we are not trying to steal the ball. All we are trying to do is maintain good defensive balance, plug outlets, and force the other team into errors. I think the team that tries to steal the ball overcommits itself, fouls too often, and does not do a basically sound defensive job. Try to force the other team into awkward situations. This will force errors and obtain the same result as stealing the ball, without the hazards listed above.

### Do a Selling Job

A coach has to do a tremendous selling job on the press to his boys. A pressing defense is a team defense. You are not only overplaying your man, but you also are playing the ball. You have to talk on defense and switch a great deal. The responsibilities are so much greater, and you therefore have to act as a unit, helping each other out.

There is a lot of coaching involved as a result of the careful attention that must be paid to every minute detail. The offensive team knows where it is going and what it is trying to do. The defensive team cannot commit itself until the offense has made its move. Therefore, the pressing team has to learn to talk; it has to get its point of vision or angle on the ball and on the players. It has to decide whether it is going to force the ball outside or force the ball inside into a trap.

### SCOUTING

A large amount of the success of a press depends upon scouting. You must have the knowledge of how the other team will react to a press. You must know what particular press will be most effective against that team.

Our pressing strategy against a team is definitely determined by scouting reports. We do a tremendous amount of scouting. We scout four or five nights a week. Because we are not satisfied with only one scouting report, we sometimes scout a team three, four, or five times. Also, to check ourselves, we will have an outside scout send us a report. We want to know exactly what the opposition will do in almost every situation. I truthfully feel that any success we have had in pressing is due to our scouting.

### MANY TYPES OF PRESSES

In today's game there are many different types of presses. There are presses that attack you full court. There are some that allow you to throw the ball in and then attack you at three-quarter court. Then there is another press that will attack you at mid-court. Also, there is the front-court press after you get into your offensive territory. There are combination presses—

maybe the top two men are playing a man-to-man press and the back three are playing a zone. Just to say a team will press doesn't actually tell much of the story. There are many variations.

## Be Flexible

Don't become known just as a full-court pressing team or a zone pressing team or a half-court, man-to-man pressing team. We like to feel that our opponents never know exactly how we will press them.

Sometimes we allow you to throw the ball in and then attack you. The next time, maybe in the same ball game, we will try to stop the throw in. My philosophy is always to keep the other team off balance and never let them know exactly what you are going to do next. We may force the dribbler outside and the next time force him inside. Sometimes you may get a full-court press—other times a half-court. It may be a zone press or a man-to-man.

We want to keep the other teams off balance. We will sometimes press early in the game just to test the other team's reaction to a press. Then at half time in the dressing room, we tell our boys how best to overcome the attack of the opposition. We might even come out the second half using a different type press. We do this because we feel that the opposing coach has been instructing his players during the half on how to overcome our first half press. Often a completely different type of press in the second half so unnerves your opposition that it has a devastating effect. When you are getting ready to play my ball club, I don't want you to feel that I am going to play you any one way. I think this is the secret of the press.

Of course you want to take advantage of the other team's weaknesses and you want to neutralize their strength. Their personnel and the particular game situation will help you determine what type of press to use. If a team has a great dribbler or a great passer throwing the ball in, we may concede the throw-in and cover that good ball-handler. Consequently, they will have a weak dribbler handling the ball coming down-court. Another time, maybe a weaker ball handler is throwing the ball in. In this case we wouldn't concede the throw in, rather we would play him tight and try to force a bad pass.

Basically, I like the man-to-man press, but when pressing a dribbling team, I would use the zone press. If a team has several good sharp passers, however, a zone press would overcommit itself and then you would really be in trouble. That situation calls for a man-to-man press. Your choice as to whether you use the full-court, three-quarter court, or the half-court press would depend upon the situation.

No matter what type press you choose, always remember to be sure you spend enough time in practice on good basic defense. If your players can't play good defense, they can't begin to press.

## FULL-COURT MAN-TO-MAN PRESS

The first thing you will have to decide is whether or not to overplay the man throwing the ball in. Then, you want to decide whether to play his receivers tight and prevent the throw-in or to allow him to successfully throw the ball in and then attack his receivers with the ball. Many teams will attack the man throwing the ball in—others will play away from him and double team the most logical receivers. Both methods can be very successful, depending upon the situation.

Next, you will have to determine how your opponents are attacking the full-court press. Do they attack with two men, three men, or do they use just one dribbler? Where do they place their other men? The answers to these questions determine how you are going to play your other men.

## Three-Quarter Court Man-to-Man Press

In this press allow the throw-in on the three-quarter court press. Then you must decide if you are going to force the ball to the sideline or if you are going to force the ball into a trap in the middle. We like to do it both ways—depending upon the situation and the personnel involved. Again, we want to know how the opposing players will be positioned. This determines the placing of our defensive players. What moves they make determines our reaction. Remember, we are not trying to steal the ball. We are trying to force an error or a jump ball situation.

## Half Court Man-to-Man Press

Some teams let you cross the mid-court line and press you at that point. We prefer to attack right at the line. We don't want you coming in too far, because with a hard dribble you can penetrate us a little too much. We want you to start committing yourself almost before you get to the mid-court line. We feel we can force the dribbler in the desired direction a little better at this point. We force both to the sideline and to the middle for the trap. We want you to throw the wild pass. And, again, we want to capitalize on weaknesses that have been uncovered by our scouting reports.

## Zone Presses

Just like all the other phases of defense, the zone press has to be adjusted to the offensive maneuvers. I don't think you can simply play a 3-1-1, a 1-2-1-1, a 2-1-2 or a 2-2-1 zone press and be successful. It depends on the other team's attack as to how you should place your men. If your team becomes known for one particular type of zone press, it will lose a lot of its effectiveness. Your opposition can spend all of its time preparing for your one and only press and do a good job of overcoming it.

When you play us you might be facing a 2-2-1 zone press one time down the floor and a 1-2-1-1 the next time down. It all depends upon how you attack our zone press. We don't use any one set-up on a zone press. I feel the team that uses only one zone press is actually giving inches to his opposition, in a manner of speaking.

## Philosophy of the Press

You have to know exactly what you are going to do when you go on the floor. I think you and your philosophy can force the other team out of its best moves. We always want to force the opposition into their secondary moves. My entire defensive philosophy is to take away the opposition's best moves, thereby taking away their offense.

Of course, you can't stop everything they do; but by capitalizing on their weakness, you are much closer to adding a game to the win column.

Basketball is much like a game of chess. We try to predetermine our moves, depending upon what the opposition is doing. As soon as they find the answer to our moves, we want to come back with something else.

Seldom a day goes by that we don't spend some part of our practice on the presses. We have basic fundamental drills that help a boy to be a better defensive player. This in turn helps him to apply the press much more effectively. We have drills that use all five men and incorporate all the ideas on pressing that we have. Then we actually practice on our pressing defenses.

It all boils down to one important fact; you only get out of something what you put into it. It takes much hard work, both on the part of the coach and of the players, to have a team feared for its devastating press.

Thirty years of coaching basketball, thirty
winning seasons. That is the perfect record
of John Robert Wooden, who received the
top accolade by his fellow members of the National Basketball Coaches
Association by being voted the 1964 "Coach of the Year" in recognition
of his bringing UCLA a NCAA championship and a perfect 30 and 0
record. He also was named "Coach of the Year" by United Press International.

# John R. Wooden

This, of course, is his all-time greatest record, but Wooden has always been a winner. First, as three-time All-State guard at Martinsville, Indiana High; then as a three-time All American cager at Purdue University; and now as a winning coach for 30 straight seasons—11 in high school ranks, 2 at Indiana State Teachers' College, and now 17 at University of California at Los Angeles.

Besides the coveted NCAA crown, "Wooden's Wonders" also swept to a perfect AAWU title with a perfect 15-0 record, won the important Los Angeles Classic tourney, and ranked number 1 in both the AP and the UPI polls.

A fantastic record for a great coach and gentleman.

8

# STOPPING THE
# FAST BREAK

John R. Wooden
Basketball Coach
U.C.L.A.

Because the fast break is such an effective offense, every team will be faced many times during the season with the problem of stopping it. Even a team that possesses personnel better suited to a ball control type of offense will, at various times during a game, find opportunities to fast break. Therefore, your team must always be prepared for these situations, no matter what type of team you may face.

## OFFSET THE STRENGTH OF YOUR OPPONENT

From my own point of view, I believe in trying to offset the strength of the opponent, or capitalizing on a weakness in a manner that will require very little adjustment in your own normal play. I believe that if you spend too much time trying to stop an opponent, it may result in a failure to develop your own potential. I am of the opinion that whenever you spend too much time worrying about the opposition, you have the danger of creating, perhaps subconsciously, a defeatist attitude in your own team. Your players will worry about the other team more, instead of letting the other team worry about them. I try to teach everything I do in a positive way, and I think worrying about the other team is a negative approach. I want the opposition to be worrying about us, rather than my doing anything which might tend in any way to make our boys worry about them.

However, I want my players prepared for anything the opposition might do, so we might change some little thing to offset their strength. I want our kids to have confidence in their own ability, but I don't want them cocky. I want them to respect everybody we play, but I don't want them to be afraid of them. I feel that sometimes when we spend too much time in discussing what we are going to do to destroy the opposition, we subconsciously hurt our own aggressiveness and our own initiative. By taking this negative approach, we are no longer going to be in charge of the ball game.

### Two Methods of Stopping the Fast Break

As far as stopping the fast break, I feel that there are many different ways of defensing it, but I think there are two that are more common. One of them deals with your actual defense and the other deals with your offense. The methods are: (1) Playing the slow game and taking the good shots. (2) Stopping the outlet pass by guarding the rebounder tightly and blocking his passing lanes.

#### PLAYING THE SLOW GAME

This deals with your offense, and it involves playing a ball-control type of game. You will handle the ball for a number of passes before attempting almost any type of a shot unless you get an absolute set-up. I feel that the main or principal purpose of this method is to attempt to control the tempo of the game.

If you can get a fast-breaking team impatient because of your own delayed offense, you may cause them to lose their initial drive or cause them to try to hurry up their break, and these things may result in more ball-handling errors and missed shots on their part.

In an effort to offset your delayed tactics, they may change to their regular style of offense or defense, which means you have placed them on the defensive. Then you have them worrying about you. Any time you have the other team worrying about you, you have gained some advantage; and you force them to depart from the style of game they want to play. Furthermore, the ball control offense, properly played, will give the opposition less rebounds from the defensive boards, where most fast breaks really originate. They will have fewer rebounds, I think, for two reasons: in the first place, you will attempt fewer shots which means there will not be as many opportunities to rebound. Also, you will be getting the higher percentage shots and hitting most of these shots. This means there will be fewer opportunities to rebound. This method also might permit you to keep two men back usually and attempt to have a little more defense against the quick break.

## STOPPING THE OUTLET PASS

The other method, in my opinion, is to try to tie up the man who gets the ball off the board, thus making it difficult for him to pass out quickly, and secondly, to try to choke off his potential receivers. If the man who gets the ball off the boards can be prevented from making the quick pass to teammates who are in an advantageous position, then I think you can, in all probability, stop the break right there. If the first pass-out is made successfully, you can still cause some trouble at times by choking off the possible pass into the breaking lane. If you force the first pass away and keep that man from passing into the breaking lane or perhaps even force him to dribble instead of passing, you have helped stop the break (Figure 8-1).

On the first pass-out, the receiver almost always will have to receive the ball with his back toward his offensive basket or, at least, his side to his offensive basket. At best, this is an awkward position at that particular moment. By hard work and practice against the man receiving that pass, you can often cause many teams enough trouble to discourage the break.

In stopping the outlet pass, we try to block the passing lane immediately to the side where we know that you are most apt to pass. In blocking the passing lane, if I can force you to lob the pass, or if I can force you to bounce the pass, I think we have stopped your fast break right there. If I keep you from making that quick direct pass out and the rest of our men do the job they are supposed to do, we are not going to be hurt on

**Figure 8-1** **Stopping the Outlet Pass.** (3) has just rebounded a missed shot by team X. $X_3$ immediately guards (3) tightly. $X_1$, $X_2$, $X_4$, and $X_5$ immediately fill the most logical passing lanes to prevent the quick pass-out and subsequent fast break.

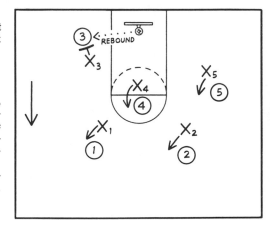

the break. We guard the man with the ball high and encourage the lob pass or the bounce pass.

There are men that are extremely good at getting the ball out quickly. In this case, we determine, if we can, where they like to pass first and try to block that up. If we feel that because of our size or some other factor we can't do a good job blocking him up immediately, then we try to see if we can't close his passing lane. In both instances we try to encourage him to throw the ball to a weaker dribbler. In other words, if he uses the outlet pass primarily, we try to cover his blocking lane and passing lane. If he is a dribbler, we try to zone him and force him into an area where he will make the bad pass.

If we play a team that has one outstanding rebounder, we may decide to assign the responsibility of guarding this player to one man, with instructions to concentrate on keeping this player from getting any rebounds—even at the expense of not rebounding himself. He just guards the boy when the ball is up on the boards and doesn't try to rebound himself. Often, to make it clear, a coach may say to the boy, "If you get a rebound yourself, unless one simply falls in your hands, you are not doing your job."

We also use spot tipping out from our offensive board and occasionally a quick press to combat the fast break. I like to use a zone press if they like to dribble that ball out. If they don't, we use a man-to-man or a combination with real hustling and defensive balance.

## OTHER THINGS TO CONSIDER WHEN PRESSING

We take many things into consideration when attempting to stop a fast break. How are they getting it out? If they can't stand pressure, we are going to try to pressure them. And if they have a certain peculiarity, which most teams do, we want to take advantage of that. For example, some board men almost always pass out to the same side of the floor after clearing the boards.

If we know this rebounder is apt to control the boards, or pretty well control them, his having that characteristic to pass to a certain spot will cause us to gamble a little bit and play toward that spot.

We know that most right-handed men take the ball going under the basket; then turn to their left, turn, cock their right arm to throw it. So we give up a little bit of the left side of the floor going down (it's our right backing up on defense), and put pressure on the dribbler's strong side. We do this because we have found through studying the pictures, charts, and so on, that perhaps 75 per cent of all their passes are going to come in to the right side. So we bunch a little more there. When we find these things out, we want to try to take advantage of them. If we know that they have some boy who likes to dribble a lot and doesn't have his head up on the pass, then we definitely try the zone press. Scouting is one of the most important factors in stopping the fast break. You have to scout them to find out what they do, so you can stop it.

Generally speaking, if the fast break is completely free lance, a team will either be a dribbling team or a passing team, and we will try to play them accordingly. My feeling is that regardless of what the offense is doing, I want a defense that hustles, talks a lot, is aggressive, and concedes nothing. I want a defense that uses common sense, good judgement, and works together. If they will do that, we will have a pretty good defense, no matter what they are doing.

## MAN-TO-MAN PRESS

Quite frequently, we will go to a man-to-man press to stop a fast break if we feel the team can't stand a press. A lot of teams will get real tough if you let them get started on you; but giving them that immediate pressure may cause them to travel in the back court, miss a pass, or hurry and throw a pass that shouldn't be thrown, thus giving your back men a chance to intercept. We feel that whenever we use the press it is completely a five-man job; and no matter how good a job your front men do, you haven't helped yourself if your back men don't do their job. So it is a combination thing, and we feel that oftentimes if your opposition has one weak link, then putting pressure on that one weak link may cause them a lot of trouble.

With my front linemen I stress constantly that they are not to try to steal the ball. They are trying to force the offense to make a bad pass that our back linemen can intercept or to force them into an error. If you start trying to steal the ball, you are going to foul. If a team is any good at all, you cannot steal the ball from them. You just can't take the ball away from a good man, but you might make him make an error. There it becomes a situation where other people have to be working with him. They may not be thinking quite as quickly as he is. They may be faking to get open when he throws the pass, or they may not anticipate like he did. If you force him to throw one or two that go astray, you may upset their whole team.

### Defensing the Fast Break When Outnumbered Under the Opponent's Goal

Sometimes, of course, even after doing a good job on the two methods of stopping a fast break, a team still will get caught 3-on-2, 2-on-1, 4-on-3, 5-on-4, or something like that.

On the 3-on-2 we like to have our top man (X1) situated at the top of the key, bluffing, hollering, making a lot of noise, and protecting primarily the strong side (Figure 8-2). In other words, if the man that has the ball or the man coming down the middle is a right-handed man, we split him on the right. We try to force the pass to the left if we can. I don't mean that we

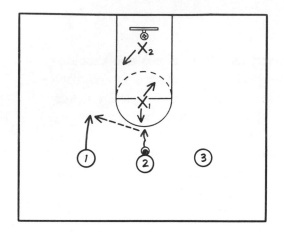

Figure 8-2 The 3-on-2 Defensive Situation.

overplay him too much, but we still encourage the pass to his left. We prefer the man getting the shot to be approaching the goal from the left side because not too many players are left-handed. We feel that we have a little better chance of making a clean block and picking him up if he gets the ball. Our defensive player at the top of the circle is bluffing and trying to stop the man out front. He will back up, but he doesn't back up much past the top of the circle. We don't want to give the offense a high-percentage shot inside. The front man is going to be bluffing, and we want the deep man (X2) to take a position about one step in front of the basket. We don't want him to stand straight in there; we want the knees flexed a little and the hips bent, the elbows bent and the fingers loose, etc. He must not make any move until that front man makes the play. If the front offensive man has the ball, our deep man does absolutely nothing except take the man to whom the offense passes. When he takes that side man, he must not permit a set-up. That is his job.

The front man has the responsibility of covering the man coming in from the other side and also the middle man that just passed off. Our main objective is to hold them for a second or so until we can get help and not give them the set-up. We must make them shoot the shot from outside. Whatever we do we don't

want that back man to go out too far after them. We realize
that two men can't keep three men from getting a pretty good
shot, but we think we should be able to keep them from getting
the set-up. That is the whole idea. Force the offense to delay
until help comes.

On a 2-on-1 when we get one boy caught back, we want him
to keep backing up and slowing them down if he can (Figure
8-3). He is retreating and not going to give up the set-up. The
only time that he would make the play, since he is bluffing primarily, would be if the man with the ball gets the ball out in
front of him and dribbles it too high, or some such thing. If our
boy sees that he can get it, he takes it. But he must be sure he
can get it when he makes the play. Otherwise, he is playing a
delaying tactic to try to force the man in front to take the jump
shot from outside or to slow down. He must not let him pass

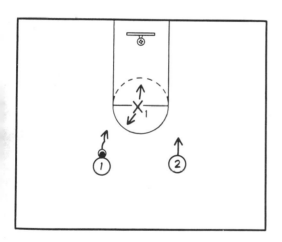

**Figure 8-3  The 2-on-1 De-
fensive Situation.**

to that cutter. We think the cutter is the dangerous man—not
the man with the ball.

If the man with the ball drives, we want to make him drive
to the weak side. That is, if he is right-handed we want him to

go left; if he is left-handed we want him to drive to his right.

On a 5-on-4 or a 4-on-3, we just drop back into a zone until everybody gets down (Figure 8-4). We still want to prevent the set-up. This situation is not as dangerous because the offense won't get as good a shot. In other words, in the 2-on-1 they

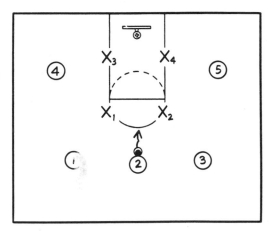

**Figure 8-4   The 5-on-4 Defensive Situation.**

should get a better shot than they should with a 3-on-2, and the 3-on-2 should get a better shot than the 4-on-3, or the 5-on-4.

Even if we have to give up the 15- or 18-foot jump shot, we have still prevented the crip shot—the bunny.

### MENTAL ATTITUDE

When you have a club that works together and has the right mental attitude, it should attain most any goal. Of course, my theory of coaching is, and has always been, never to mention winning. I never mention it. Never! Now that is a hard thing to believe when some say winning is the main thing and the only thing. Don't misunderstand me—I like to win as much as the next fellow, and there is nothing wrong with it. If a kid did not play to win, I would just as soon not have him. But I never mention it. I constantly preach to our kids that all I want them to do is to be able to say at the close of every practice and at the close of every game, "I did my best."

I tell our kids that when the game is over I never want to see their heads down. If they did their best, the score doesn't amount to a lot. It just doesn't mean a thing—if they did their best. If they won and didn't do their best, they don't have anything to be proud about. I want their heads up. So I never mention winning in any way. When I talk to my players before practice begins, I will say, "There is just one thing to do today boys, and that is to improve yourselves."

Henry P. Iba, the director of athletics and
coach of basketball at Oklahoma State
University, has been one of the nation's
leading figures in baskétball for many years.

Iba's basketball teams at Oklahoma State University have won 573
games and lost 219. He coached Maryville High School in Missouri and
the University of Colorado in the five years before he came to Stillwater.
His over-all collegiate record is 685-241 in 34 seasons, one of the nation's
few mentors with more than 600 victories.

# Hank Iba

Born August 6, 1904 at Easton, Missouri, Iba attended Westminster at Fulton. He was inducted into Missouri's hall of fame in 1961. Coach of the year, Helm's All-Time Hall of Fame, and many other honors have been accorded him.

Hank Iba produced two NCAA champions in basketball, one runner-up, three more NCAA finishes of fifth or better, and had an NAAU runner-up at Maryville. He has produced 13 All-Americans at Oklahoma State University.

9

# ATTACKING
# THE PRESS

Hank Iba
Basketball Coach
Oklahoma State University

## Reasons for the Press

In discussing the press in basketball, I feel we should first discuss the reasons for it being used as much as it is today. I think there are two reasons why we are seeing the press more than we ever have in basketball.

First, it is used because of a lack of good defense being taught in the high schools and colleges. In other words, we get a boy that is not fundamentally sound enough to play a good zone or a good man-to-man. We find that it takes us too long to teach this boy to play the type of defense we want, so we compensate by using the surprise methods of defense which we call the press, or pick-up. This surprise element is the big reason we see the press so much in today's game.

Secondly, I think that we practice offensively too much on one end of the floor and that we don't play up and down the floor enough; so, naturally, the press is more effective than if we work daily from one end of the floor to the other.

The press is here to stay. It will increase, and there will be different types. Basically, there are only two types of presses in basketball today: (1) zone and its variations; (2) man-to-man and its variations. But coaches are already developing a combination of these two. In attacking any press, you must keep your offense simple so that it will work against any type of press or any combination of different presses.

## THE PRESS IS MAKING US COACH BETTER

The press is making us coach better because it's making us organize our practice sessions better. Any success against a press comes from good organization of practice in which you work day after day until the boys feel that they can master the press. It's impossible to attack the press on a day's notice or even on a week's notice. Attacking the press must be incorporated into your offense. Start working on it early in the season—even on the very first day of practice.

You want to gain confidence, along with good ball-handling and good timing, against any type of press. This cannot be accomplished until each lad is sure of himself and has confidence in himself. Day-to-day practice will bring this speed, deception, and confidence. Then, it is a matter of beating the full-court press—keeping in mind that you must also spend enough time on the half-court press so that you can take care of that situation too.

Personally, I don't believe that any team can press full court consistently and be successful against a team that practices over 90 feet of court. I do think it is possible for you to disrupt a lot of ball clubs with a full-court press regardless of its style if they haven't practiced against it.

Your first problem is· to be sure to discourage the pressing team in back court by showing them you have the knowledge of your play. They will then try to pick you up and bother you at the middle of the court. Then, you must be in a position to operate with an offense from half court on into the basket area. That will take the press off you and put your team into a shooting position.

Each coach is aware of the fact that we are going to have a great many different types of presses at various places on the floor. It is a matter of us having an offense that is a part of the coach. In turn, he makes it a part of the player. Then, we practice until it becomes natural and until we can play under game conditions without getting excited. In this way we get the best from each individual. However simple your play might be, it takes constant practice. To me the strength of the press lies in the other team's lack of practice against it and the effect of the surprise element on the individuals playing against it.

## To Beat the Press

1. Look for the press every time you take the ball out on the defensive end of the floor. This takes the surprise element out of it.
2. Any time the press is on, don't be satisfied to just get the ball across the center line. Try to score—not taking wild shots but, again, not slowing down and trying to run a set offense either.
3. Simplify your press offense. You meet many different kinds of presses. Have a press offense that will work against almost any kind of press.

## How Oklahoma State Attacks the Press

The following diagrams illustrate what attacks against the press have proven to be most successful for us. Figures 9-1a through 9-1e show what we do after crossing the mid-court line. This is our attack against either a zone press or a man-to-man press. Figure 9-2 illustrates our movement to get the ball down the floor against a man-to-man press, and Figure 9-3 illustrates our movement to get the ball down the floor against a zone press.

### ATTACK #1 (FIGURES 9-1a – 9-1e)

We use a high-low or tandem-post offense after crossing the mid-court line. Man number 4 is our point man; 2 and 3 are

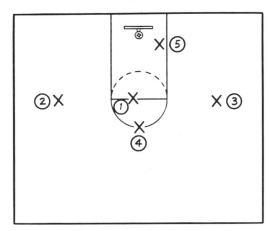

**Figure 9-1a Press Offense Positions After Crossing Mid-Court Line** (both against zone press and man-to-man press.)

our wing men; number 1 is our high post; and number 5 is our low post. Numbers 3, 4, and 2 can interchange positions as the occasion demands. Numbers 1 and 5 can also interchange positions, but they are never in the outside positions. They are either on the high or low post. After the ball crosses the mid-court line, we follow four options. We refer to these options as *hold, cut, pick,* and *go away.* Players 4, 2, 3, and 1 have these options. The only man that we do not give the options to would be the low post man, number 5. He would not be in a position to use the four options. Remembering that every player but the low post has these options, we will use man number 4 as an example. Number 4 may hold the ball and dribble until he has a good shot from the one-on-one situation (Figure 9-1b). Number 4

**Figure 9-1b Hold Option.**

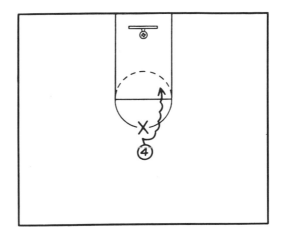

can pass and cut, either using number 1 as a screen or cutting directly for the basket and on out to the strong-side corner (Figure 9-1c). Number 4 can pass and pick either 3, 1, or 2

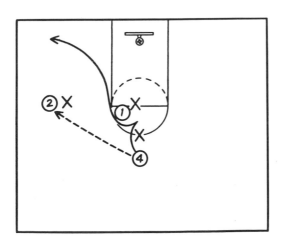

**Figure 9-1c Cut Option.**

(Figure 9-1d). Or number 4 can pass and go away (Figure 9-1e). On this option we prefer number 4 to come over the top

Figure 9-1d   Pick Option.

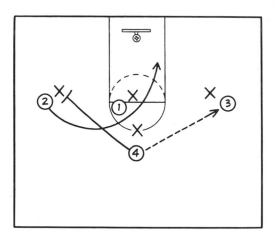

of the high post so that he will definitely show that he is going away. The important thing to remember is that the first receiver has the same options as the man that started the play. Likewise, the second receiver has the same options as the first two preceeding him, and so on.

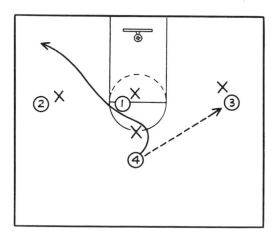

Figure 9-1e   Go-Away Option.

## ATTACK #2—AGAINST THE MAN-TO-MAN-PRESS (FIGURE 9-2)

We like to have a set position of our men any time we get the ball out of bounds, whether it be after a made field goal or free throw or after a violation by the opposition. Our men are positioned as illustrated in Figure 9-2. We always start our movement with the man on the same side of the floor as the ball (number 3 in Figure 9-2). We do not say this man must take a certain

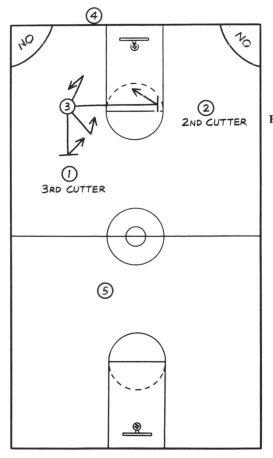

Figure 9-2 **Attack Against Man-to-Man Press.** Movement to get ball in-bounds and downcourt against a man-to-man press. Man on side of ball is first cutter.

position or perform a certain movement every time, but we do require that he does not come to the corner to receive the ball. Number 3 has the options of starting down-floor and cutting back toward the ball; moving to the ball and cutting back down the floor; going across and screening for number 2 and rolling back; or he may do the same thing for number 1. In case we can't hit number 3, he goes on down the floor to the opposite corner. Number 2 is the second cutter, and he has the same options. If number 2 doesn't receive the ball, he goes to the opposite corner down-court, and number 1 becomes our third cutter. In any event, against a man-to-man press, we want a one-on-one situation when bringing the ball down the floor. We want everyone but the man with the ball to clear and give him room to bring the ball down. Meanwhile, number 5 has moved down the floor into the low-post position.

The one thing we must be sure of is that men 2, 3, and 4 are interchangeable on the defensive end of the floor the same as they were interchangeable in Attack #1. We are trying to set an offense that will tie in to Attack #1 with continuity. These are the movements that have been most successful for us.

### ATTACK #3—AGAINST THE ZONE PRESS (FIGURE 9-3)

We set our men in the same positions that we did in Figure 9-2. Number 4 takes the ball out of bounds; numbers 2 and 3 line up half the distance between the free-throw line and the sideline; number 1 lines up somewhere near the mid-court line; and number 5 would go on down the floor and be in a position to meet the ball coming across the ten-second line. The two things we are trying to do against a zone press are: (1) get the ball to number 1 in the middle; (2) then pass off to either wing man cutting down the sides and from the wing men pass to number 5 on the offensive end between the jump circles.

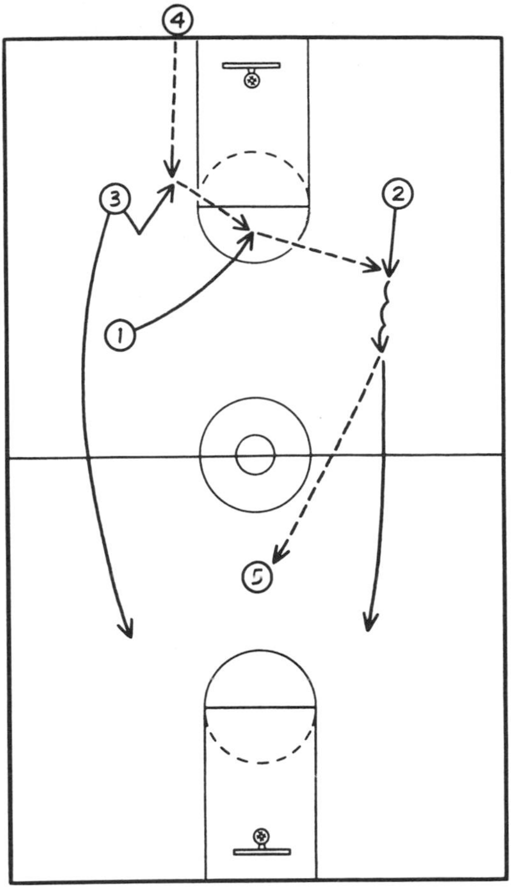

**Figure 9-3** **Attack Against the Zone Press.** Movement to advance ball against any kind of zone press. (4) passes to (3), who has gotten open. Man (1) cuts to middle and receives pass from (3). (1) passes to (2) cutting down sideline. (2) passes to (5) who is between the jump circles. (3) and (2) continue down sidelines for possible return pass from (5). (4) is the trailer.

You must keep in mind in Figure 9-3 that you want your players to visualize the center jump circle as the basket on the offensive end. Your idea is to work safely into the center and then continue into the baseline offensively. By doing this, I think you will take away a lot of the doubts and hesitations on the part of your players in practice.

To conclude, always remember to have a trailer against a zone press. You'll save yourself from letting the opposition get several cheap baskets. This could be the difference between a win and a loss. And whether it be a man-to-man press or a zone press—*attack it*. This can be accomplished only through constant practice.

*159*

Facing a major college schedule each season, Ken Norton has completed 18 successful years as head basketball coach at Manhattan College. For 7 of the past 12 seasons, Norton-coached teams have participated in post-season tournaments—the National Invitation Tournament in New York on five occasions and twice in the National Collegiate Athletic Association Tournament. In 1957, the Manhattan "Jaspers" became the first New York area college team to win the annual Holiday Festival Tournament in Madison Square Garden.

# Ken Norton

As president of the Metropolitan Intercollegiate Basketball Association, the Manhattan coach served as chairman of the National Invitation Tournament selection committee 1959-1963. He has also served as a member of the Eastern College Athletic Conference's executive council from 1955 to 1959 and is a former member of the National Basketball Rules Committee.

Coach Norton is a past president of the Metropolitan Basketball Coaches Association and was a director for several years of the New York *Journal American* Basketball Clinics conducted at Madison Square Garden. He has participated as a guest lecturer at many basketball clinics for players, coaches, and officials.

# 1 0

# *SPECIAL SITUATION PLAYS*

Ken Norton
Basketball Coach
Manhattan College

Since there are so many different situations that arise in today's game, it is virtually impossible to have a special play to cover each situation. I believe in having plays to cover three basic situations; and then through good organization, perfecting these plays to cover a multitude of situations.

## THREE BASIC SITUATIONS

The three basic situations for which we have special plays are: (1) tip-off plays, (2) in-bounds plays, (3) stall plays to protect a lead late in the game.

We have plays to cover each of the three situations, and we spend our time perfecting these plays rather than having many different plays for many different situations. We realize that we will be scouted and that our opponents will know what we are going to do in each situation. However, through good organization of our practice sessions, we intend to have our boys attain such a high level of ability that it doesn't make any difference whether the opponents know the plays or not. Our plays will still be successful because our boys have practiced long enough and hard enough to insure their success.

## A Common Error—Over-Coaching

I base the above coaching beliefs on the fact that we college coaches get so many boys that are over-coached. I have had players that used as many as eight different offenses or defenses while playing high school ball. We have trouble getting them to perfect one basic offense or defense.

I believe in keeping everything simple and getting true organization on one attack before you try to branch out and teach others. I realize a lot of coaches feel their team can pick something new up, and because of this element of change, they might get results sometimes. But I wonder if it really pays off over the long haul.

When I first started coaching, I went through the same thing until I woke up and realized I was over-coaching. My boys were just half-way learning everything I taught them and were not perfecting any of it. This was when I decided to simplify everything so that the few things we did run, would be perfected and run well.

## Simple, Yet Fluid

Of course, in our basic plays the boys have options they can run. In other words, we don't want to take away the initiative of the player. As they perfect the play and their own individual moves, it gets stronger and stronger.

I'm sure many of my opponents who have played me year-in and year-out find they don't even have to scout us, and, yet, you can speak to the same opponents and find out how hard it is to stop us. It all goes back to the idea of keeping everything simple and maintaining a great fluidity in your attack. This is what I try to get across at the various coaching clinics.

## ILLUSTRATIONS

The following diagrams illustrate plays for each of the three basic situations. Keeping in mind the material on hand and his players' strength, a coach can pick one or two best suited for his team and, through practice, attain a high level of ability with his choices.

### TIP-OFF PLAYS (FIGURES 10-1—10-6)

**Figure 10-1 Center-Jump Play.** Center (C) tips ball to (4) and cuts right downcourt. Meanwhile, guard (2) has cut left downcourt. (4) can pass to (C) or to (2) for the basket. (5) sets partial screen on defensive center, $X_3$, and (1) stays back for defensive coverage.

**Figure 10-2 Stealing the Tip with the "Clock."** When tip is insecure, all four players rotate counter-clockwise. Anticipation and timing are required. (5) attempts to cover both $X_4$ and $X_5$; (4) covers $X_1$; (1) covers area between $X_1$ and $X_2$; (2) covers area between $X_2$ and $X_5$. Players must be careful of circle violations. Players automatically switch if "steal" fails.

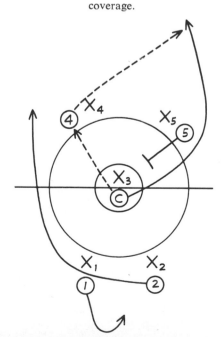

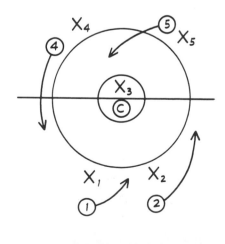

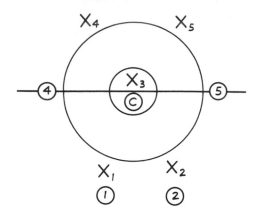

**Figure 10-3** **Defensive Center Jump Positions.** To protect loss of ball. Also set up a strong screening outline for the protection of a deep back tip or diagonal back tip.(1) and (2) contest $X_1$ and $X_2$. (4) and (5) protect against fast break by $X_4$ and $X_5$.

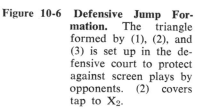

**Figure 10-4** **Defensive Center Jump Formation.** Offers excellent defensive possibilities and a positive set-up which insures possession if the jumper (C) can tip the ball back in defensive territory. (1) and (2) can screen opponents leaving (4) to secure the ball. If ball is secured, (C) may be able to break free with a screen from (5).

**Figure 10-5** **Jump Formation— Possession Play.** (1) tips to (2), who hands off to (5), cutting for the basket. (3) and (4) stay back for defensive balance.

**Figure 10-6** **Defensive Jump Formation.** The triangle formed by (1), (2), and (3) is set up in the defensive court to protect against screen plays by opponents. (2) covers tap to $X_2$.

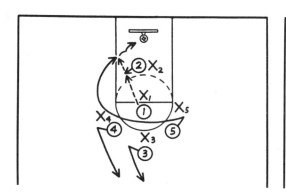

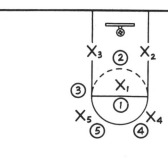

## IN-BOUNDS PLAYS (FIGURES 10-7a—10-10)

**Figure 10-7a Spinner Play.— Option #1.** (3) feints toward ball. If $X_3$ reaches to prevent pass from (2), (3) spins away and cuts to basket for a bounce pass from (2). (1), (4), and (5) keep their defensive men busy with fakes and feints.

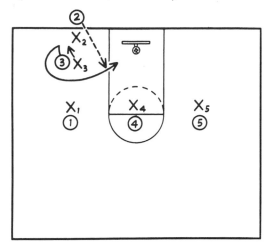

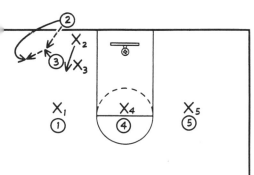

**Figure 10-7b Spinner Play— Option #2.** (3) gets pass from (2). (2) cuts outside of (3). If defensive man $X_2$ slides through, (2) sets for shot.

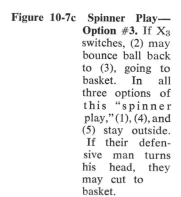

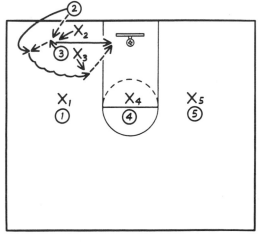

**Figure 10-7c Spinner Play— Option #3.** If $X_3$ switches, (2) may bounce ball back to (3), going to basket. In all three options of this "spinner play," (1), (4), and (5) stay outside. If their defensive man turns his head, they may cut to basket.

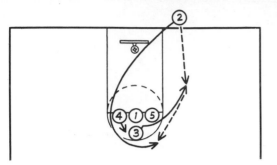

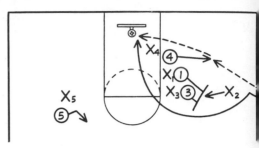

**Figure 10-8 Out-of-Bounds Under Basket.** (2) takes ball out. (4), (1), and (5) form triple screen at foul line for (3). (3) cuts to baseline, trying to rub his man off on (5). (3) can shoot the ball or pass to (2) who has cut around behind same triple screen. If (2) can't pass to (3), (4) backs up for long in-bounds pass from (2). Regular offense is then set up.

**Figure 10-9a Out-of-Bounds on Side —Option #1.** (3), (1), and (4) stagger their post. Big man should take second spot. (2) cuts off double screen after passing ball in to (4). If free, (2) receives pass from (4).

## IN-BOUNDS PLAYS (*Cont.*)

**Figure 10-9b Out-of-Bounds on Side —Option #2.** (3) clears out immediately after (2) goes by him. (1) moves over to set a screen for (4). (4) drives off (1) with a dribble for the shot. If X₁ switches, ball is passed to (1) who has turned and moved toward goal.

**Figure 10-10 Out-of-Bounds on Side Midcourt.** Moves must be quick. The basic objective is to get the ball in play. The big man (1) button-hooks for the outlet pass in case (4) is in trouble with the ball. (3) may break free with help by a screen from (2) for a lay-up shot.

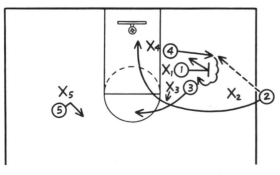

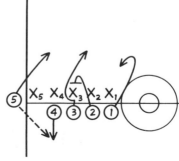

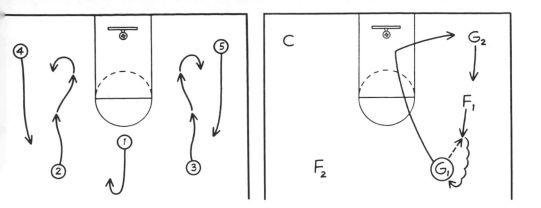

**Figure 10-11**

**Stall Play.** Players use entire area of forward court. (2) and (4) keep interchanging positions on one side and (3) and (5) on the other side. Center man (1) button-hooks up and down middle, relieving teammates of ball when forced. Change-ups and long cuts to basket are the continuity. Only a lay-up shot is attempted. Once a player stops his dribble, he must get rid of the ball.

**Figure 10-12a**

**Sideline Stall.** $F_1$ breaks up sideline and gets pass from $G_1$ (pass outside on sideline). $F_1$ takes $G_1$'s position; $G_2$ takes $F_1$'s position; and $G_1$ takes $G_2$'s. Repeat. Keep (C) (Center) out of it entirely if possible.

## STALL PLAYS (FIGURES 10-11—10-13)

**Figure 10-12b**
**Sideline Stall Alternate.** $G_1$ can't pass to $F_1$ so he passes to $F_2$ who has cut for basket and back out. Then $G_1$ and $F_2$ trade places and run stall as in previous diagram. $F_2$ is the next best dribbler after $G_1$, $G_2$, and $F_1$, who are your three best dribblers.

**Figure 10-13**
**Three-Man Freeze.** (1) dribbles toward the right as (2) starts a hard cut for the basket and reverses. (1) passes to (2). The center of of the court is kept free. The change-up can often be used to break free for easy lay-ups. (2) dribbles toward the left and passes to (3). (3) has cut down the left sideline before retreating to get the ball. After passing to (3), (2) cuts for the right corner to replace (4). The corner man is alert to help out at any time. (4) and (5) wouldn't come out unless absolutely necessary.

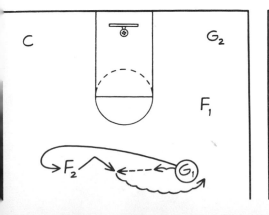

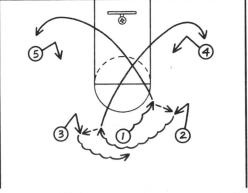

Brian McCall, a native of East Palestine,
Ohio, has just concluded his seventh year
as head basketball coach at the University
of Maine. His Maine basketball teams have compiled excellent records,
winning four Maine State Series championships and two Downeast Classic
titles.

The Maine mentor has been recognized by fans and officials for his
high standards of conduct on and off the court. His players are encour-
aged not to protest decisions to officials, and Maine has ranked among
the nation's leaders in fewest fouls committed per game.

# Brian McCall

His personal honors include an invitation by the schools of New Brunswick to conduct clinics in that province, a "New England Coach of the Year" award in 1961 by the Bangor (Me.) Daily News, and three invitations to contribute to books or national coaching publications.

He was graduated from Dayton University in 1949, where he captained the basketball team, and received his master's degree from Ohio State in 1951. He coached highly successful Ohio high school teams from 1949 to 1958 and was named coach of the year on one occasion.

# 11

# *CHARTING AND SCOUTING*

Brian McCall
Basketball Coach
University of Maine

## CHARTING

One of the less glamorous aspects of coaching is keeping accurate charts. It is very important because these charts give an indication of the progress being made by the team and, in some cases, by the individual. However, there is no use charting if it is not going to be done 100 per cent accurately.

I feel that a coach should keep to the essentials when charting. He should have a purpose in mind and keep his charts to a minimum. Do not use a particular chart simply because you read about it in a coaching book or because some other school in your area uses it. A chart should be made with a purpose that fits the individual need of the particular team or coach.

## WHO SHOULD KEEP CHARTS?

I suggest that either the managers, jay-vee basketball players, or perhaps loyal helpers in the booster club can do this while the varsity game is going on. Actually, you need a minimum of four people to chart the game. One boy can chart the turnovers, one the rebounds, one the jump balls, and one boy on the shot charts.

**Figure 11-1 Game Chart.**

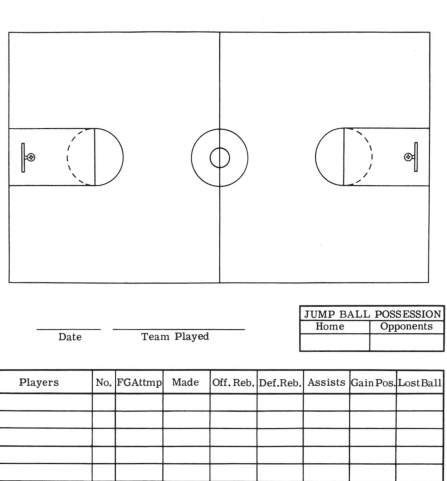

_____ _____
Date                    Team Played

| JUMP BALL POSSESSION | |
|---|---|
| Home | Opponents |
| | |

| Players | No. | FGAttmp | Made | Off. Reb. | Def.Reb. | Assists | Gain Pos. | Lost Ball |
|---|---|---|---|---|---|---|---|---|
| | | | | | | | | |
| | | | | | | | | |
| | | | | | | | | |
| | | | | | | | | |
| | | | | | | | | |
| | | | | | | | | |
| | | | | | | | | |
| | | | | | | | | |
| | | | | | | | | |
| | | | | | | | | |
| | | | | | | | | |
| | | | | | | | | |
| | | | | | | | | |
| | | | | | | | | |

| Opposition Floor Errors |
|---|
| |

| Opposition Rebounds | |
|---|---|
| Off. | |
| Def. | |

More people, of course, could help and, maybe, add to the accuracy by giving each one a smaller assignment. You could have one boy on your team keeping the shot chart for your team and another one for the visitors. In the turnovers, you could have one boy just keeping bad passes, another the double dribbles, and still another the walking violations. In regard to the rebound chart, you could have one boy keeping maybe three or four of your players and the other one keeping two or three of your players. In other words, the more people you have charting for you, the better coverage you will receive. What we are striving for is greater accuracy. Figure 11-1 shows a combination chart which can be used if you have only one person to do your charting.

## GAME CHARTS

### SHOT CHART

First, we will take the game charts—the type of charts that might be kept while the game is on. One which is obvious would be the shot chart. We want to know how many shots the team takes, the spots where they take them, and what positions on the floor most of the scoring is done. We can take this shot chart for the team and break it down into an individual shot chart after the game is over. I like to have this chart given to the opponent at half time so he has a chance to see from where both teams are shooting and scoring. I expect the same treatment when I go to the opponent's court.

Some coaches do not use the shot chart. They feel some of their players will think another player is hogging the ball and taking too many shots. The coach confronted with this problem can, after the game, take his team shot chart and break it down into individual charts and give them out to his team members.

In this way each boy knows how many shots he took, from where they were taken, and how many he missed. He doesn't have to compare his shots with someone else's unless he wants to.

## TURNOVERS

Another chart that I feel is important is what I call "turnovers." This includes the bad passes, the double dribbles, and the various other floor errors that caused you to turn the ball over to the opponent. We have the ball only so many times, and when we have it, we would like to score a basket. Therefore, we don't want to turn over the ball to the other team. I feel that a chart of this type is vitally important to show the boys where they are making these errors, and why we are not scoring more.

## REBOUND CHART

A rebound chart is vital because it is the type of shot—the percentage shot—that we have to prevent the other team from getting. We have to get the rebound after they get one shot. You can't stop a team from shooting once, but you must try to stop them from getting the second and third shots. In order to do this, you must be able to rebound. The rebound chart is very important in teaching your players how to rebound.

## JUMP BALL CHART

Another chart that I feel is very important is the chart that tells you how many jump ball situations there were during the game and how many times your team gained the ball during these situations. This chart is sometimes overlooked because many coaches don't realize how often jump-ball situations occur during the ball game and how important it is to secure possession of the ball in these situations.

## OFFICIAL'S CHART

The last type of chart we use during the progress of the game is the official's chart. The Eastern Collegiate Athletic Association, of which we are a part, passes out a card on which we chart the official after the ball game is over. On this chart are many things that we look for, such as appearance, knowledge of the rules, mechanics, manner of handling the players, calls under the basket, calls on blocking or charging, calls on traveling violation, judgement, courage, etc. We rate the officials on a point basis of one through ten.

## PRACTICE CHARTS

### FOUL SHOT CHARTS

Now we go to the practice charts. I like to keep a list of ten foul shots that each boy shoots at the end of practice and how many he makes. Each boy shoots ten fouls against an opponent. We chart this and use a type of ladder tournament where we put each boy's name on a long, thin sheet of paper about six inches long and about two inches wide. We put these along our bulletin board, and every night each boy knows against whom he is going to shoot the next night. When you lose, you drop down and go to the end of the line. You have a new opponent every night. We shoot ten fouls in this manner—two boys at a time—and we put some sort of pressure on each player. I believe this method results in getting more work done in fewer shots because the boy is concentrating on each shot.

Of course, in our score book we have records of how many times the individual players go to the foul line and miss. I feel this should also be put up on the bulletin board in the form of a chart. The percentages of each boy and the percentages of the team should be kept up-to-date.

## TWENTY-ONE

We play a game of twenty-one before practice begins. Each player shoots a set shot from out in the floor and then a jump shot from back of the foul line. The set shot counts two points and the jump shot one point. We have the defensive man rebound the long shot and throw the ball back to the shooter back of the foul line. Then he takes his jump shot. In other words, the set-shooter never follows his shot in—he just slides over to some position back of the foul line where he can shoot the jump shot. The defensive man who has his hand up while the boy is shooting the set shot will rebound and throw it back out for the jump shot. The boys do this until the shooter scores 21 points.

## ONE-ON-ONE CHART

The last chart that we use in practice is one in which we play a one-on-one each night. The big men—the men who play with their backs to the basket—will play one-on-one at the top of the circle or down on the low post. The small men will play one-on-one anyplace outside, usually in the middle of the court about a foot above the top of the circle. They play until a total of 20 points is scored.

## SCOUTING

It is far more important for a coach to scout if he plays a man-to-man defense than if he plays a zone. People who play the zone like to scout, of course, but you could possibly go into a game blind if you are a good zone team and get away with it, since you have to know more about the other team if you are playing a man-to-man defense. This is one thing to think about in scouting. I know of one team that actually used the zone because they couldn't go out and scout. They felt that, of the two defenses, you wouldn't have to scout nearly as much or as thoroughly using the zone as you would with a man to man.

## MAKE YOUR OWN SCOUTING FORM

Of course, not everyone is looking for the same information when they scout, so I feel that a coach should make up his own form when he goes out scouting and not just take the standard form that he may get from some other coach. He should take that form and improvise on it. When you go out to scout, your form should suit your purpose. In charting and scouting there is no set way of collecting information; it all boils down to this question: What are you looking for for your team? (Figure 11-2 shows a sample scouting chart. The game chart shown in Figure 11-1 should be used to supplement this chart.)

Now I feel that we can break scouting information up into several basic items, no matter who you are—college, pro, or high school. I feel that there are some basic things that we are looking for: (1) Physical Facilities (2) Team Characteristics (3) Individual Characteristics (4) Information on the officials.

## PHYSICAL FACILITIES

The first things I look at when scouting are the physical facilities of the gym. I like to arrive at the gym even before the teams come out for their warm-ups. I also like to sit in the middle seats —up high to get a clear view. This gives a clear view and arriving early allows me to check these facilities. Is the lighting good or are there dark spots on the floor? I have known of coaches who,

**Figure 11-2    Sample Scouting Report.**

Teams: _____ vs. _____

Date: _____

Place: _____
　　　　　　(Gym)
　　　　_____
　　　　　　(City)


Physical facilities:

　　Light:  Good _____  Fair _____  Poor _____

　　　　　　Blind or dark spots on floor?  If so, where?


　　Size of floor:  Standard _____  Other _____

　　　　　　If "other," what are its dimensions?


　　Scorer's table and scoreboard:

　　　　　　Are they within easy reach and sight of the visiting bench?
　　　　　　If not, what measure could be taken?


　　Backboard:  Shape _____

　　　　　　Made of:  Wood _____  Glass _____  Other _____
　　　　　　Mounting:  Free standing _____  Mounted on balcony _____  Other _____

Team characteristics:

　　　　Offense:  Patterns being used (please diagram)
　　　　　　　　Also chart:
　　　　　　　　　　Out-of-bounds plays
　　　　　　　　　　Jump ball plays
　　　　　　　　　　Shots taken (made - missed)
　　　　　　　　　　Fouls

　　　　　　Tendencies:
　　　　　　　　Patterns run to the right _____
　　　　　　　　Patterns to the left _____

　　　　　　Adjustments:
　　　　　　　　Do they adapt their pattern to the defense they face?

　　　　Defense:  Zone? _____  Man-to-man? _____  (If zone, please diagram)

Individual characteristics:  (Please keep shot diagram)

| No. | Pos. | FG Attempted | FG Made | Dribble L R Dr. | Pass | Screen | Comments |
|-----|------|--------------|---------|-----------------|------|--------|----------|
| 18  | F    | 10           | 4       | G F P           | FAIR | NO     | GOES WELL TO HIS LEFT, GOOD LH JUMP SHOT |


Officials:

| Name | Comments |
|------|----------|

after scouting in a gym and discovering inadequate lighting, have practiced in their own gym with several lights turned off. These coaches wanted to get their players used to the different lighting.

I also want to know the size of the floor. This can affect your game, especially if you are a running team or a pressing team. Some coaches actually put tape down to cut the floor size down to suit the floor on which he is going to play. You want to check where the players' bench is in relation to the scorer's table, so that the boys can report without any trouble. If the gym has only one clock, I want to sit where that clock is looking right at us the second half.

The backboard is another physical facility we like to scout. Is it fan-shaped? Is it square? Is it glass? Is there a balcony behind it? Just what is behind it—what type of background? In some places, the fans actually hang over the top of the board, and you would want to legislate against this when you go to play the game.

## TEAM CHARACTERISTICS

The next item I feel that every coach is looking for in some degree is team play—some information on the team. I feel that the coach should first check the team play as closely as possible. Of course, by having gotten there early and having looked at the warm-up drills, you have already found out what shot each boy takes, from where he takes it, and some of his individual moves. In the warm-up most boys will usually shoot from the spot on the floor that they are going to use in the ball game, and you can get a pretty good indication there what type of shot the boy has. I want to look for team play, especially at the beginning of the first half and the second half. It is in the first half, at the beginning of the ball game, and beginning of the second half that they are going to play as a team. They are going to try, in the first few minutes, to do what the coach has been coaching and teaching them. This is when I will get their team pattern, rather than waiting until the middle of the game. We check the team play, patterns, offense, and defense right-away. Of course, we are charting. We chart the out-of-bounds plays, the jump balls, the offensive pattern, where the boys play on the floor, and just what type of pattern they are trying to use. We take a shot chart to tell us which portion of the court this team shoots from the most. We get an idea of whether they are strictly a right-handed or left-handed team; that is, whether most of their patterns are initiated down the right or left side of the court.

Of course, we note team defense at the beginning of the game. If it is a zone, we want to know who plays where in the zone and how they move when the ball is rotated in different areas. So, we are actually looking for team situations. We haven't broken anything down to individual moves yet in the first few minutes of the game. We look closely for this team play, out of bounds plays, and jump balls, offensive and defensive patterns.

As you watch them play, ask yourself a few questions: Are they in shape? Can you fast break them? Can they be pressured? Can we zone them? Are they a good passing team? Is it better to play slow or fast against them? Will an aggressive man-to-man bother them? Will they always fast break if they get a chance? Do they have floor balance on offense? Can they press or play a good zone? What, if any, is their big weakness?

### INDIVIDUAL CHARACTERISTICS

Then we go to the individual. Here we look for physical characteristics and playing habits. We will already have an indication of the player's shooting ability and where he shoots from during the warm-up before the ball game. I like to know where on the court this boy plays the most. Does he just pass the ball, or is he a shooter?—I especially want to have this bit of information. If he is one of these fellows who works the ball around and feeds the other players, we will ignore him whenever he shoots. If he is just the fellow who presses the button on the offense, we won't guard him. In our style of play, we will just keep our hands off of him. We never assume that all five players can score. We want to see if they really shoot and can score.

## SCOUT THE OFFICIALS

We even scout the officials every chance we get, because we are liable to get these officials in a ball game. We want to know if they have favorite calls or if they allow contact, etc. The E.C.A.C. encourages us to scout officials because they are interested in finding out the ability of the official. Therefore, when we are scouting a game, we scout the official and turn a card in on him.

## CONCLUSION

Now, I will again emphasize the basic things I think every coach should look for: (1) physical facilities, (2) team characteristics, (3) information on the individuals, (4) something about the officials.

When scouting, we like to watch the game and do the writing in-between quarters or between halves. We like to observe and keep a mental picture. Of course, people who have been in basketball long enough can do this and get a mental picture of the game. They like to eliminate writing while the game is going on, if possible. Of course, we chart out-of-bounds plays and jump balls while the game is going on, but the other writing is kept to a minimum until we have a good chance to do it.

If you can't get to the ball game to scout, check the sports pages of your newspapers. I know of one high school coach in a big metropolitan city who was going to the state tournament. He was playing a team from the southern part of the state that he had not had a chance to see play during the year. He went down to the public library and got out the home-town newspaper of this team and read all about them from the start of the season to the end. By doing this, he had a pretty good idea of what they had been doing all year long. Of course, it is a good idea to keep a file on the teams you play by clipping their write-ups out of the newspapers during the season.

Last but not least, it is also a good technique to scout a game by taking a tape recorder with you and talking into it during the course of the game. There are many ways to scout, and I have tried to show some of the many things to look for when scouting. Always remember that scouting wins the close games. Remember, too, that you are working when you are scouting. Sometimes it's easy for several coaches scouting the same game to end up in a "bull session" during the game. This kind of scouting won't win the close ones.

John W. Bunn was basketball coach at
Colorado State College from 1956 to 1963.

Bunn was graduated from the University of
Kansas in 1921 after having won 10 varsity letters in football, basketball, and baseball—a record that still stands at the Kansas institution.
After graduation, Bunn was appointed an instructor at Kansas and was
assistant coach. He earned his M.S. degree from Kansas in 1936. While
at Kansas, Bunn worked under "Phog" Allen, the noted Kansas coach,
and Dr. James Naismith, the inventor of basketball.

# John W. Bunn

In 1930, Mr. Bunn went to Stanford as professor of physical education and head basketball coach. He remained in that position until 1938 when he became Dean of Men. At Stanford, Bunn developed several outstanding players, such as All-American Hank Luisetti, and guided the Indians to the mythical national title in 1937.

Bunn was Director of Athletics at Springfield College, Springfield, Massachusetts, for ten years prior to coming to C.S.C.

He is permanent chairman of the National Association of Basketball Coaches Hall of Fame Committee, editor and national interpreter of national basketball rules, a past president and secretary-treasurer of the National Association of Basketball Coaches, past member of the NCAA basketball tournament selection committee, and treasurer of the Basketball Federation of the United States of America.

Bunn has also taken on the responsibility of investigator for the infractions committee of the NCAA since his retirement from Colorado State College.

He has traveled in Europe, Australia, the Far East and all over the United States conducting programs pertaining to the game and its rules.

# 1 2

# *WINNING*

# *BASKETBALL*

# *STRATEGY**

John W. Bunn
Basketball Coach (Ret.)
Colorado State College

* John W. Bunn, *The Basketball Coach*: *Guides to Success,* 1961, by permission of Prentice-Hall, Inc., Englewood Cliffs, N.J.

Coaches are constantly required to make decisions quickly during the course of a game. The plan of play has usually been worked out in advance; but, often, conditions change and altered plans are necessary. The success with which these changes are made may mean the difference between victory and defeat.

When and how should time-outs be used? When and for what reasons should one substitute? When and under what conditions should a pressing defense be used? When should a team freeze the ball? When is the fast break indicated? When should ball control be employed? When should offensive and defensive tactics be changed?

Each game and each situation has varying factors so that it is not possible to cover every one in a specific manner. If this were possible, most of the thrill and chance would be taken out of the game for both the coach and the players. Also, different coaches may analyze and react to a given situation in a different manner. The philosophy and background of the coach will partly determine his moves. Also, the preparation of his squad and the available personnel are conditioning factors.

There are, however, general guides which may be helpful.

These will be presented. Actual examples will be given to show the implementation of these guides.

### Frustrate Your Opponent

An over-all guide for governing play against an opponent is to employ those tactics which are most aggravating and frustrating. Another way to state this principle is, "Play the way your opponent does not want you to play." In order to be able to implement such a principle, it is necessary to have a team and its players trained in versatility. Unless one prepares his team and players in practice to execute many types of tactics, it is asking too much to expect them to employ new tactics on the basis of directions given during the progress of a game. Even though the tactics may not represent the type of game one plays best, they will nevertheless be profitable if they tend to disorganize and disarm an opponent.

Strategy of this kind presupposes an accurate knowledge of the opponent as well as of the philosophy of the coach. Thorough scouting reports provide the former; and a knowledge of the background of the coach and the observation of his methods over a period of time provide the latter. With this information, a period of several days prior to a contest may be spent in rehearsing the tactics to be used against an opponent. Most teams adopt a definite pattern of play from which they cannot deviate with success. For this reason, preparation of this kind can be carried out to great advantage.

### Strategy for the Individual

The following are examples of strategy which show how this philosophy of play has paid dividends by turning possible, even sure, defeat into victory. Each represents an actual case, but games and teams are not identified in order to avoid the appearance of criticism of a coach or the embarrassment of a player. Most are from recent games.

1. In a recent NCAA play-off game, the star of one team seemed to score at will; and this team left the floor at half-time with a comfortable lead. This occurred despite the fact that the team had been scouted, the tactics of this player had been thoroughly analyzed, and a plan had been devised and practiced for stopping him. He had developed the habit of faking in one direction and then moving in the opposite before going up for a jump shot with which he was deadly accurate. The star was so quick and effective with these tactics that opponents were afraid not to move with his fake for fear he might move in the direction of the fake. This was true of the player in this game who was assigned to stop the star during the first half. But during the second half, the guard made the correct moves and stopped the star without a field goal. Not only that, but he stole the ball from him several times, completely upset the poise of this star player, and caused him to press so badly that he became a detriment to his team and had to be removed from the game. Needless to say, the team that had been in the lead at the half lost the game in the last minute of play. Here is the case of a player who was stereotyped in his habits of play and an opponent who did what this player did not want him to do. The outcome of a game hinged upon this kind of strategy.

2. A similar situation is the case of a star player who was averaging close to 30 points per game. The team of this player usually was sparked by its star. One opponent decided to concentrate on this one player at the risk of letting others on the team be unguarded. The concentration on the star held him to three field goals and permitted a team that would have been beaten with comparative ease to win by more than 20 points.

3. In another NCAA tournament game an offensive star who was a weak defensive player was continually maneuvered into a position where he was forced to cover a player driving for the goal. In a short while, he had been charged with four personal fouls. As a result, he was forced to let offensive players dribble to the goal unguarded for fear he would commit his fifth foul and thus be lost to his team for his offensive value for all the game remaining. Here is a case of capitalizing on a known defensive weakness of a star scorer.

4. A star of some years past was a terrific dribbler with driving speed that prevented most opponents from guarding or stopping him. It was observed, however, that he had developed the habit of dribbling only to the outside. A guard was instructed to overplay to the outside until this player demonstrated that he could dribble successfully to the inside. The result was that the effectiveness of this player was completely erased. He tried to move inside but without success. Completely unorthodox defensive tactics were employed, but they accomplished the purpose. The player was prevented from doing what he wanted to do. He was so conditioned to a single maneuver that he was unable to change.

These are examples of employing the principle of "preventing a player from doing what he wants to do." These examples can be multiplied without end but are undoubtedly sufficient to indicate the possibilities and to stimulate one's imagination so that he can make adaptations and devise strategies in other or similar situations.

## TEAM STRATEGY

The following are a few examples of the application of the same principle in situations of team play that may be helpful to the reader.

1. One of the top teams in the country was stopped by a relatively weak team. This was done by tactics designed to offset the strength of the opponents, who had built all of their offense about their top-ranking center. This team had been so successful in its single-post attack that it had not found it necessary to resort to another type of play. Its attack always started after the ball was fed to the post; and gambling on this bit of observation, the weak team played to prevent the ball from getting to the post by playing in front of the post and sagging another defensive player to a spot behind the post. This trick so surprised and frustrated its opponent that the weaker team was victorious by a margin of a single point whereas previously it had been beaten by 20 points. The amazing part of the play was the fact that the single-post team continued to try to force the ball to the post throughout the game, only to have it intercepted time after time. Evidently this team became so conditioned to this one pattern of play that when an effective defense was set against it, either it could not believe it was stopped or it was unable to change its tactics. This, of course, reveals weakness in a team which lacks flexibility in its attack. Most teams, however, at some time fall prey to inflexibility.

2. On another occasion, a team with four players over 6'6" had designed its attack so that no shots were taken except close-in shots developed from a double-post offense. This planning was meant, of course, to utilize the dominating height of its four big players. A small team (with only one player as tall as 6'3"), in addition to running this big team, employed a defense that always placed a player in front of and behind each big man at the basket. The defense would drop off the man with the ball on the side or in front and give this man a free shot rather than permit the ball to be passed into the basket. Surprisingly, this big team refused the outside shots and continued to try to work the ball in closer to the basket. They were beaten by 12 points.

Toward the end of the game, they tried outside shots, but they were so conditioned to their other type of play that, although the players were in advantageous positions, there was no confidence in outside shooting and, thus, no effectiveness.

3.  In a quarter-final NCAA game some years ago, a team was known to use the usual attack against a zone defense—to stand still and try to out-pass the defense. A team which was not particularly adept at playing a zone started the game with its customary man-to-man play but soon found itself unable to cope with the driving offensive play of its faster opponent. It went into a zone, which immediately caused its opponent to change its offensive tactics to a standstill pass pattern. As soon as this occurred, its opponent went back to its man-to-man play, but this was never discovered because of the standstill tactics. As a result, the game became a close contest and, although the weaker opponent did not win, it had the opportunity and lost by only a very small margin.

4.  A team with a versatile attack in which any player could play in any position was playing a team which had a tremendous rebounder of 6'9" and a speedy, clever "ball hawk." This team was winning its games by the use of a lightning-like fast break started by its great boardman and by interceptions from the clever work of its "ball hawk." The team was using a man-to-man defense. To offset this advantage, its opponent revolved its offense until the rebounder was playing out in front and the "ball hawk" was in the rebounding position. This stopped the fast break, prevented interceptions, and made an even game out of what otherwise would have been a walkaway.

5.  Many teams resort to ball-control tactics. Such teams seldom, if ever, use the fast break. They prefer to maneuver the ball until their opponent makes a mistake on which they can capitalize. Every move of such a team is made according to pat-

tern. If permitted to play its own game, such a team will look great. Its play will be as smooth and regular as the movement of a clock. It will hold down the score and spectators are likely to comment erroneously on the great defensive strength of this team. If, however, it is not given time or opportunity to set its own pace and pattern, it will usually fall apart. It is so much easier to play slowly and deliberately than to play fast and aggressively; moreover the deliberate team is unable to adjust to the faster tempo of play, and it becomes erratic.

The most striking example of the efficiency of this kind of strategy was an NCAA final. A perfect ball-control team was ignominiously defeated when its opponent resorted to forcing tactics and to a fast break.

6. One year, a National Invitational Tournament final was won by the reverse tactics. A normally fast-breaking team realized that it was no match if it played its opponent's game. It had one very good ball handler, so it got the ball to him after every exchange of control and he literally slowed the game down to a walk. He would actually walk as he dribbled from the back court to the front court. No shots were taken until the ball was worked in for a comparatively close-in shot. As a result of this strategy, it was able to keep pace with its bigger and faster opponent and won the game at the end.

These last two examples not only illustrate the validity of the philosophy of not permitting a team to play the way it wants to play but also the advantage to the team that is able to dictate the pattern and tempo of the play.

7. A ball-control team is seldom as well-conditioned as a pressing, fast-breaking team. So, in addition to upsetting the poise of such a team by forcing it to play a type of game it does not want to play, it is possible to run the ball-control team down before the end of the contest. The results may not show until

late in the second half; but in the end the difference in condition becomes evident, and it is surprising how a large divergence in the scores can be erased in a very few minutes. The opponent becomes not only tired but also erratic.

The writer has had several experiences that demonstrate the effectiveness of this type of strategy. There were two opponents, one on the East Coast and one on the West, which seldom, if ever, won a game against this type of strategy in spite of their superior talent. Year after year and game after game, these opponents would have what might appear to be a commanding lead at the end of the first half, only to lose, sometimes by a wide margin, at the end. The advantage of fast play, fast break, and full-court pressing is that the opponent cannot avoid playing a fast, hurried game. If he is not in condition and is not trained to play fast, eventually he always suffers as a result of fatigue which causes erratic play and ineffective shooting.

On another occasion a team that was pressing and fast-breaking was behind throughout the game (as much as 24 points in the second half, and 11 points when there were just a few seconds more than two minutes to play); yet it won the game with a shot that went through the basket as time expired. Old man fatigue was finally a factor and spoiled an opportunity for great jubilation by the tiring opponent.

8. A change of tactics on the spur of the moment to counteract a move by an opponent or to meet a situation that arises suddenly during a contest requires that the coach follow the moves of his opponent attentively at all times. Three illustrations of game situations will illustrate this point:

    a. In a two-game series it was found that the pivot could operate at will. All play was directed to him in the first game and, as a consequence, he was able to score over 30 points. In the second game, the opposing coach strengthened his defense at this position by dropping off of the ball at the side to prevent a pass to the center. The side man was not a scoring threat but a strong rebound player and fast.

To thwart this bit of strategy by the opponent, a player who was an excellent shot but very slow was substituted for the side man with instructions to shoot every time he got the ball until his opponent came out on him so that he could pass to his pivot. The defense continued to sag so that the substitute scored four times in succession. This was sufficient to open up the pivot again so play could proceed as in the first game.

b. In another game the pivot man had carried the burden of scoring. He was very accurate in this particular game so the team was instructed to capitalize on his scoring by getting the ball to him whenever possible. The game was a see-saw affair; and with 45 seconds to play, the score was tied, largely through the efforts of this pivot man.

Time was taken out with the ball in control of his team. It was reasoned that since the pivot had been the effective scoring threat throughout the game, the opponents would logically conclude that the ball would be passed to him for the last shot. Consequently, the play was set to pass to the pivot in order to concentrate the defense on him and then to have him pass off to another player for the final shot.

The ball was controlled until the last few seconds when this strategy was executed. It worked as planned so that the player who made the final shot had an unhurried opportunity. He scored, and the game ended as the ball went through the basket.

c. Scouting reports indicated that a team had strong outside shots but that they needed plenty of time to make their shots. When this point was further proved during the progress of a game, the defense was changed suddenly from a massed defense around the goal to a pressing defense. The outside players not only were stopped from scoring but they also became hurried and erratic in their play. The tide of the game was completely changed from an even contest to a rout.

## SUMMARY OF STRATEGY

The foregoing examples of actual play situations may be summarized to cover strategy in general as follows:

1.   Force your opponent to do the things he does not want to do. Players and coaches often become confused and even panicky when their normal pattern of play is blocked.

2.   Try to set the pattern of play by forcing your opponent to play your game. Outstanding teams can be tricked into this kind of play.

3.   Substitute only for tactical purposes. A particular game situation requires a player with a special talent. A good shooter is needed at a particular moment. A strong defensive player is needed to stop a star. Rebound strength is needed. A regular in a particular game may not be playing his usually strong game so that his substitute is better at winning. A whole team may be "off" so that all efforts to get them to play have failed. The substitution of a whole new team is indicated.

It is seldom wise to remove a player for making a mistake. To substitute under such circumstances will tend to destroy confidence, and it may destroy the effectiveness of a conscientious player for the rest of the season.

4.   Take time out for tactical reasons only. Time-outs for injuries are not included here because these can be cancelled

by substitutions. But if an opponent scores three times in succession without a counter score, it is wise to call a time-out in order to analyze the situation and make changes in play as may be indicated. The brief interruption of the game often stops the scoring spree.

If a team becomes erratic or disorganized, time should be called in order to recoup and to get play reorganized. A complete change of tactics may be indicated.

In a particularly evenly contested game, if a weakness is discovered in the opponent's play, a time-out to plan to take advantage of the weakness may change the whole complexion of the game.

In the second half, as the game reaches its crucial stages, it is wise to call a time-out to make plans and to make sure that all players understand the strategy to be employed.

So far as possible, a team should save its time-outs for the second half.

Time-out should never be taken to rest.

Time-out should never be requested by the team that is dominating the play or that is in a scoring spree. Let the opponent use his time-outs in these cases.

5. Pressing tactics have value in many situations and can be employed effectively at many stages of a game; but there is no fixed rule to determine when to use them. The fact that a team is a dangerous pressing team often is sufficient; and though the press may not be used, the fact that an opponent is expecting it at any moment can have a demoralizing psychological effect.

Pressing is always effective against a slow or inexperienced team. It can be used against such teams at any time and until complete mastery of the game is obtained. Against a strong team, varied tactics should be employed. In any case, it is usually more effective to alternate pressing and regular play, to alternate full-court and half-court press. This prevents a seasoned team from adjusting to the defense readily. Giving this team a steady diet of pressing will permit it to organize effectively to meet it. If the press has been used effectively against such a team and it takes time-outs to organize, it is good strategy to call off the press for a few minutes and then re-employ it. By such tactics, the value of the opponent's time-out to reorganize is often lost.

The press is effective merely to change the tempo of the game and to disrupt the planned play of a team. In this respect it can be used at the beginning of and toward the end of the first half, at the beginning of the second half, and in the early minutes of the last quarter of a game. One should never wait until the last few minutes to employ the press, because it takes time for the results of a press to show. Therefore, using it in the last moments of a game usually amounts to desperation tactics, the admission of defeat, a so-what attitude; "We are beaten so we may as well try the press." If the press has value, it should be used in a positive way. It has no value as a lost cause. The psychological effect of the press on the players is demoralizing when thought of in this fashion. The press has value to get one's own team moving on nights when both the offense and the defense are lagging. Moreover, to encourage individual initiative, surprise pressing tactics are excellent strategy and take advantage of a team that has been lulled into a state of complacency to the extent that it becomes callous and inattentive in handling the ball in the back court and in the front court in front of the defense. These tactics are best used after a team has been conditioned to a retreating or passive defense.

6. Much of what has been written about the use of the press may be said of the fast break. A team may use the fast break as a basis of its offensive play or it may use it whenever the opportunity presents itself. The mere threat of a fast break is often a sufficient deterrent to cause an opponent to play cautious

and conservative offense. A championship was won in this way, when a coach was so fearful of the fast break of his opponent that he permitted only one man to rebound after a shot. The others stopped back on defense immediately after a shot. The opponent, of course, had little opportunity to fast-break but the threat of its lightning-like fast break was just as effective.

7. Ball-control tactics have a definite place in basketball. When a team is badly outmanned with respect to size, its only hope after the defense is set is to control the ball until it can secure a good, unhurried shot. Its chances of securing the rebound, if the shot is missed, are very limited. It is good judgment, therefore, for this team to control the ball until it can get a shot at a position from which its chances of scoring are as great as possible.

The employment of ball control under these circumstances is legitimate because the team is positive in its efforts. It is working to get a good shot, not necessarily a lay-up. It is not holding the ball and refusing to shoot to hold the score down. Such tactics are never to be condoned. They represent a defeatist attitude that is not good for the players and is certainly not good for the game. It makes a farce of it. A coach who would teach this type of play is a detriment to the game, and he should be severely censured.

Ball control employed strategically as indicated is a definite part of basketball. It is one of the main reasons why a time limit should never be introduced into the amateur game. It may be used effectively, also, to help a team smooth out its play. When a team becomes sloppy, erratic, and uncoordinated, it can recover its smoothness and coordinate its movement by a short period of passing within its pattern before attempting a shot. Teams which employ a continuity of movement find this tactic very helpful.

8. Freezing tactics—controlling the ball when the team is

ahead but there is no intention of taking a shot—should never be employed. Usually used toward the end of the game, their purpose is to pull the defense out and away from the basket.

Such tactics usually destroy the offensive effectiveness of a team and give it a negative attitude. To use such tactics when a team is scoring and has built up a lead usually puts it back on its heels and causes it to lose its scoring touch.

There should always be the aim to score and to keep the team offensive-minded. When a team is ahead at the end of the game, it should work for a lay-up shot only. At the other stages in the game, it should work for either lay-up shots or shots when the shooter is poised, balanced, and unhurried. But, always, there should be the objective to score.

9. Defensively, it is good judgment to mass the defense about the goal against a team that has no shooting strength outside but handles the ball well and has good inside shots. The same strategy should be used to stop inside strength under any circumstances.

10. Always plan defense in order to stop the offensive strength of the opponent, even at the expense of weakening the defense at other spots. Some coaches reason that one must concede the star his points and stop others. This hardly seems logical in view of the fact that a team invariably looks to its strength for its inspiration. If this is stopped, the chances for victory would seem to be much enhanced. One of the examples given earlier was in line with this type of thinking.

11. Offensively, a team should direct its attack at the weakness of its opponent's defense. This weakness, if it exists, may be in an individual or it may be in the pattern of the defense itself. One of the examples of an NCAA game related earlier demonstrated how one team employed this tactic.

# INDEX

*203*